COUNSELING AT THE CROSS

USING THE POWER OF THE GOSPEL
IN CHRISTIAN COUNSELING

COUNSELING AT THE CROSS

USING THE POWER OF THE GOSPEL
IN CHRISTIAN COUNSELING

H. Curtis Lyon

Second edition, 2011

Northwestern Publishing House
1250 N. 113th St., Milwaukee, WI 53226-3284
© 1991 by Northwestern Publishing House
Published 1991
Printed in the United States of America
ISBN 978-0-8100-0353-8

TABLE OF CONTENTS

PREFACE

The gospel of the Triune God is a gospel of full and free forgiveness. God has declared the sins of the world forgiven for the sake of Jesus Christ, by his life, death and resurrection. This declaration of universal justification is the central doctrine of Scripture and the essential tool in the hands of every Christian no matter how God provides the opportunities to use it.

The Lord's saving work begins with his law that prepares the human heart for the presentation of the gospel. Without the law the gospel means nothing, because people won't know they are sinners or will be content with some other way of dealing with their guilt. For example, people can try to ignore their sins; they can attempt to justify their actions; they can deny their sins. Furthermore, people suffer personal physical or emotional distress because of guilt. Most of us can think of numerous examples of the kind of pain and suffering that results from it. The law cuts through all the alternatives and exposes unresolved guilt. It convicts sinners no matter what they have done and no matter how they have chosen to deal with their guilt apart from the gospel. The law convicts all people of sin and clearly defines disobedience to God.

When the law convicts the human heart and produces genuine sorrow over sin, God has good news. Jesus' work is that good news. Jesus paid for all sin on the cross. Nothing else can give the kind of peace God's verdict gives for Jesus' sake.

Satan uses many cheap imitations of the gospel to trick people into thinking they have peace and security when they don't. In other words, Satan wants people to think sin is resolved when it isn't. The media are more than willing to offer "do-it-yourself" methods for finding peace of mind that deceive many into thinking they are handling the real problems of life when they are not. Only the gospel provides the "real thing," resolution of guilt. Christ has taken all our guilt on himself. That's why the gospel works to resolve it. Christ takes our guilt away.

Pastors and teachers have the privilege of using the law and gospel every day. They usually share the gospel with a group of people at the same time. Sometimes, however, the law and gospel can be most effectively communicated one to one. Many pastors, teachers and individual Christians know that is true. Either way, for groups or individuals, the divine word is God's tool that every Christian needs to resolve guilt.

Sharing the word of God on an individual basis may be a time-consuming way to present it. Furthermore, a pastor or teacher may find it particularly difficult to look a single person in the eye and speak the law and gospel to specific sins. Nevertheless, such individual applications have some rewards that can't be duplicated any other way. For example, we are likely to develop a deeper reliance on God, his power and his word, when we see how helpless we are without God's word to change the mind (produce repentance) of a troubled person. We will probably appreciate more the gospel of forgiveness for ourselves when we can share the good news with someone else.When the gospel produces the peace God creates, we also share the joy the angels of heaven experience over one sinner who repents.

No matter how many negatives seem to indicate that individualized application of the law and gospel is too difficult, too time-consuming, too ineffective, too taxing, the rewards still outweigh all the negatives. In addition, whether we like it or not, whether we feel competent for it or not, whether we have the time for it or not, we have the responsibility to address the specific needs of the individuals in our churches.

Without a doubt, we can always learn to communicate more proficiently with our people. It's important that we continue to improve. To do so will take some study, some experience, and some knowledge of our people and their needs. Most important, the work requires a commitment to God and his word, because he produces his results through the word. God's word and the love of God it proclaims provides the motivation and the message for doing and improving this important work.

Just as we can improve our communication skills when addressing groups of people large and small, we can also improve our skills when addressing individuals. This book will try to show how. THE DOCTRINES PRESENTED ARE NOT NEW. Thank God for that. But the reader will want to look for new and helpful ideas as we address ways of finding sin and the problems it causes in sinners, of defining the problems and the sin behind them, confronting them, and resolving the sin problem.

Christ forgave all sin, every sin. Because of Jesus' work, no sins exist on the world's record even though millions reject God's pronouncement of universal justification in Christ. Through faith, that gift of forgiveness becomes ours and our people's. Through faith, the guilt is resolved and the problems it causes are relieved. The purpose of our counseling, then, is to build faith through the application of the word of God and to arrive at the resolution of various guilt problems and their related distress. Improving that skill is what this book is about. To the extent that goal is realized, to God alone be the glory.

ACKNOWLEDGMENTS

Pastoral counseling can be time-consuming, physically and emotionally demanding, and sometimes frightening. Counselors and counselees alike can forget the power, the love and the faithfulness of God to accomplish his will and produce the peace that passes all understanding. Some may have more talents, interests or inclinations than others to do this kind of work. Where a desire for greater proficiency exists, however, additional training, experience and assistance are invaluable. I would like to acknowledge some of those people who have helped to shape the counseling portion of my ministry.

No institutions of higher learning can provide the satisfaction of experiencing the power of God the Holy Spirit at work through his word. I thank God for allowing me to see that power at work in the lives of the people I have had the privilege to serve. I thank him for the successes he has given to the ministry of his word in personal application and for the lessons I have learned from my own mistakes and failures. I thank him for the humility he produces to depend on him alone to produce the fruit, when my own weaknesses, ignorance, blindness and pride would stand in the way of his work. God alone can show us our sins and lead us to our Savior. God alone can provide the forgiveness we preach first to ourselves and then to others. All my experience prompts a humble dependence on God to give the increase.

Genuine Christian counseling cannot be done at all without the foundation of the word of God. I am indebted to the Wisconsin Evangelical Lutheran Synod for my pastoral training in the inerrant Scriptures that provide this foundation. The summer quarter at Wisconsin Lutheran Seminary in Mequon, Wisconsin has provided valuable additional tools for this work. Readily available workshops and seminars also have helped me improve my skills at counseling with God's word.

In addition, other classes were available that neither challenged nor ignored my commitment to be a communicator of the gospel first and a counselor second. One teacher in particular, Maria Pappas Nicholas, PhD, was very helpful. She acknowledged my theology and never challenged it, though she did not share it. I respect her willingness to respect me and my position. In addition I appreciate her skills in providing counseling techniques and an understanding of current psychotherapies on the postgraduate level.

Most of the additional training I was privileged to receive came through firsthand experience. This experience in many cases would have been overwhelming if it were not for resource people in the professional community. Dr. Terrence Moisan, MD, has been by far the most helpful resource. His medical expertise and his willingness to share medical knowledge, to assist in diagnosing and treating problems, and even to treat some of the people I have counseled, when medical attention was necessary, has been an invaluable part of the learning process. During all of this, his commitment to Christ and the pure word of God has given a great deal of reassurance that the work we have done has been done competently.

In the field of psychology, Dr. Dennis Jensen and the late Dr. Ben Joshel have allowed me to participate in counseling serious emotional difficulties. They have provided diagnostic testing when it was appropriate. They have explained terminology and assisted in diagnoses on numerous occasions. Again, all this was done with a respect both for the word of God and my ministry.

In the psychiatric setting I have received assistance and cooperation from several psychiatrists, particularly at the facilities of Old Orchard Hospital in Skokie, Illinois, St. Joseph's Hospital in Joliet, Illinois, Ingall's Hospital in Harvey, Illinois and Our Lady of Mercy Hospital in Dyer, Indiana. As long as a mutual respect for the distinction between their work and mine existed, full cooperation was always available. I recognize and respect the tools available to the medical field. They are gifts of God. That respect has invariably been returned to me in my ministry.

In the area of substance abuse, Dr. Gregory Blevins, PhD, has given generously of his valuable time to assist in diagnosis, treatment planning and encouragement. Dr. Blevins teaches substance abuse counseling at Governor's State University in University Park, Illinois. He is a Christian, committed to the power and authority of the word of God and the ministry of that word, while also making his professional expertise available in connection with congregational counseling.

Finally, I would like to acknowledge with deep appreciation those people who have trusted me to help them deal with the emotional, psychological and mental problems they have faced. In their difficulties they turned to the real source of resolution for their problems, the word of God and the love and power it proclaims. To them and especially to those who have allowed me to use their situations as examples in this book, I am deeply indebted. Their names and sometimes portions of their counseling have been changed to protect confidentiality. In all cases reported, however, the essentials of the development of the treatment have been preserved.

Nothing can improve on the essential tool, the word of God, with which God himself has equipped us to do his work by the power of his Holy Spirit. Only our expertise in communicating God's word can improve, to give God's people all he wants them to have. Thank God for forgiving our shortcomings. Thank God for the motivation and the channels to improve. To him alone be the glory.

INTRODUCTION

Pastor Emerson is a young, well-trained theologian. He serves St. Peter's Ev. Lutheran Church, a middle-sized congregation in a suburban area. Pastor Emerson does a consistently faithful job of keeping the members firmly grounded in the word of God. His sermons always reflect that faithfulness. He has been serving St. Peter's for just over five years, his entire ministry.

Recently Pastor Emerson has noticed a slight shift in the emphasis of his ministry. His people have increasing confidence in him, so they talk with him privately about their personal problems more frequently than they did when he first graduated from the seminary. He spends more time counseling, but he isn't always sure how to handle the problems his people are having. Many seem to be physiological or psychological problems, not the kinds of spiritual problems Pastor Emerson was trained to handle. He wonders, "What do I do about problems like that?"

If he recommended a psychologist, what would his people think of him? How would that reflect on God's call to trust in him to provide? Would Pastor Emerson still be able to satisfy the spiritual needs of his people?

Could a psychologist recognize spiritual needs in his absence? Would a psychologist help or hinder the pastor in the work he was called to do? Would the people think a human being could give them more than Christ could give?

A case in point was the time Mrs. Manning came to him. She was forty-five years old. She was depressed. She wasn't talking about a few blue days. Her depression had been going on for several months and was taking a physical toll. She saw her doctor, but he said her problem was just "nerves." Mrs. Manning didn't expect Pastor Emerson to do anything that her doctor couldn't do, but she desperately needed help. She wasn't satisfied with her doctor's answer.

"The reason I wanted to talk to you, Pastor, is that I think I need some kind of counseling. I don't know whom to see. I think I'm going crazy. I thought you might have dealt with problems like this before. I thought you might be able to help, or maybe you might know someone who can." Pastor Emerson had talked with people who had similar problems, but he had never experienced anything quite this severe. Pastor Emerson had to decide whether to handle the matter himself or refer to a counselor or psychologist. He thought and prayed about his problem and Mrs. Manning's for a long time.

Pastor Emerson knew of Christian counseling agencies nearby, but he wasn't sure about the doctrinal position or the competence of the people at the agency. He was afraid a counselor might tell Mrs. Manning something that would conflict with his own work and responsibility to the word of God. Besides that, what would happen if Mrs. Manning found relief with counselors who weren't really "Christian"? What if she traded temporary relief for the genuine comfort of God's word?

Pastor Emerson decided to handle this situation himself. He was a pastor and nothing else. He was not a doctor, and he didn't try to be an amateur psychologist. His tool was the word of God, and he was determined to apply it to Mrs. Manning's difficulties.

"Mrs. Manning, I can tell you feel bad, emotionally and physically. I know you want to do something about it and I'd like to help you with what you need to do. The best thing I can do is to tell you something you already know very well. As bad as you feel, God's love for you hasn't changed one bit since Jesus went to the cross to die for you. God has the power and the love to be able to make everything work out the best way. He never forgets your welfare, now or for eternity. I know you believe that. You've been faithfully listening to the word of God and receiving his sacraments for years. You know the strength and comfort the gospel has given you. Your faith is being tested right now, but God isn't going to let you face this alone. Just think about all that again."

Mrs. Manning did think about it seriously. She prayed. She felt a little better for a while, but essentially she felt that Pastor Emerson had let her down. She was as unsatisfied with his answers as she had been with her doctor's diagnosis of "nerves." She was unsatisfied because neither the doctor nor the pastor had bothered to find out why Mrs. Manning was depressed. Neither one had any real way of communicating with her about her problem because they didn't find out what her problem was. They both talked about symptoms, but essentially that was all they did. Without understanding what was behind the depression, all they could do was talk around the problem.

Mrs. Manning started looking for books on depression and didn't have any trouble finding a wealth of them in both secular and Christian bookstores. She practically became an expert on the problem of depression, but Mrs. Manning was not in a position to make an objective analysis of her own problem and choose the appropriate solution. The solutions to the problem of depression came from people who had dealt with hundreds of people like her. They were "authorities." Most of the material she read was Christian, or at least it wasn't unscriptural, but it didn't have as much meat as Pastor Emerson's sermons. On the other hand, Pastor Emerson's sermons didn't address her problem. Neither did his personal contact with her.

Unfortunately, Pastor Emerson's faithful preaching of law and gospel didn't relate to what Mrs. Manning was going through. Her problem and his solutions never met. The other authorities she heard and read did speak to her problems, but not with Christ's solutions.

Eventually Mrs. Manning saw a psychologist. He told her that most of her problems stemmed from unresolved guilt, but, in fact, he didn't know how to deal with guilt. He told her she would be better off if she didn't hear or think so much about it. She decided the best way to avoid hearing about guilt was to avoid church. When that happened, Pastor Emerson faced his worst fears. The faithful pastor knew his parishioner was doing better emotionally, but her spiritual condition was becoming a far more serious problem. She didn't need her God or her church anymore.

This scene may or may not sound realistic or familiar. Many pastors could simply say, "I wouldn't have handled it that way." But, if it sounds at all realistic and familiar, please don't stop reading. Pastor Emerson could be any one of us. He couldn't have been equipped better theologically, but he could have found better ways to communicate the unchanging truth of God's word.

That you have chosen to read this book indicates that you care about improving your own competence in counseling with God's truth. The difference between this book and most of the others you might read lies in the commitment to the essential truths of the gospel to be the real healing agent. Furthermore, unlike the popular pastoral counselor, Jay Adams,[1] the writer does not believe that mental, emotional and personal problems are purely spiritual, leaving no room for physical or mental factors. The writer does not believe that the professional and medical communities cannot be valuable resources. Rather, the purpose of this book is to suggest ways to use these resources while maintaining that real healing can come only from God through his gospel.

When people experience an obvious medical problem like surgery, we attend to them with the comfort of God's power and love to watch over everything and everyone involved. We can do the same thing with the word of God where emotional pain is involved. The question is *how*. The title of this book suggests that God's work through the gospel, the good news realized at the cross, is not finished until the problem is resolved, in other words, when Christ's peace reigns. We know what unresolved guilt is by experience. Christ's work resolves it. That is the gospel of resolution. By definition and by example we can learn what it means to understand the resolution the gospel provides. We can learn how to communicate the peace the gospel gives, how to recognize when we have communicated it effectively and how to maintain that resolution when God has worked it. That is counseling at the cross.

God-willing, you will find the material presented here valuable and interesting. But written material cannot

---

[1] *Competent to Counsel et alii, passim.*

replace two essentials. First, nothing can replace the power of God working through his word to accomplish what he decides to accomplish. Second, no material is of any value if you are not interested in or courageous enough to meet your people individually and to work with them out of concern for their spiritual and emotional problems.

No one has magical answers for counseling problems or counseling competence and success. The results belong to God if counseling is to be genuinely Christian. You wouldn't be reading this book if you didn't want to do all you could to communicate the law and gospel more effectively to your people. If that describes you, may God bless this effort and yours. He is the only one who can give the real blessings Christ won.

CHAPTER ONE
WHAT IS GOSPEL RESOLUTION?

The central teaching of our Christian theology is God's declaration that the world is forgiven of all sin for the sake of Jesus Christ, because of his life, his death and his resurrection. Jesus' work of redemption is universal. Every sinner can be told unquestionably and unconditionally that his or her sins have been forgiven. God's work in Christ is a completely finished product.

Faith in Jesus makes that gift of God's grace and its accompanying blessings ours. God isn't waiting for us to believe him so he can tell us he forgives us. He has forgiven us and he also creates the faith to believe it. His word and sacraments are the means he uses to do all this. The gospel is the only tool God has given us to create saving faith and to impart the peace it gives. Any peace that falls short of the peace God gives is only a temporary delusion.

Jesus gave his disciples the Great Commission of Matthew 28. He had the authority to equip and commission them for the work of preaching forgiveness because he had already won the forgiveness of sins. He said he would always be with them. He provided the

1

means, namely, his word and sacraments, to make more disciples.

Jesus' commission hasn't changed and never will. The church's work is to make disciples with the tools and with the power Christ provided. The methods and opportunities may vary, but the work, the power and the tools never will. When Christians are doing Christ's work, they are making disciples. That is as true in Christian counseling as it is in any other aspect of Christian work.

To put our work in slightly different terms, we might say that Christ wants Christians to share the forgiveness he earned for all people. He does everything else from start to finish. All his people do is "preach the good news to all creation." How will people ever get to know the good news about Jesus? The answer is simple. We tell them. We can give it to them when dozens or even hundreds or thousands are assembled at once. We can give it to them one at a time. The important thing is that we give it *to them*.

On the first New Testament Pentecost Peter and the other apostles preached the gospel to thousands of people gathered in Jerusalem. The Holy Spirit brought three thousand of those people to faith that day. Peter preached both the law and the gospel pointedly in his sermon recorded in Acts 2. He told the people gathered in Jerusalem that they were responsible for the death of Jesus. They had condemned and crucified an innocent man. Not only that, they murdered the Son of God, the Messiah. Although hundreds and perhaps thousands denied, ignored, ridiculed or otherwise rejected what he was saying, his message was directed to everyone. It was specifically designed to present the law to the multitude so he could ultimately present the gospel to them.

Peter informed the multitude that all the things that happened to Jesus were part of God's plan to save the world. The message was universal, but Peter recognized the needs of a unique audience. He addressed the law and the gospel to their situation. Even though thousands of people were present, the message was uniquely designed for that particular audience.

Peter was an expert at preaching the law and gospel because he had practical experience. He was a sinner who needed forgiveness and received it in a special way from Jesus himself, who understood his special needs. During the Savior's suffering, for example, three times Peter had said he didn't know who Jesus was. Peter needed forgiveness and he received it when Jesus met him after the resurrection by the Sea of Galilee. Peter had to face his sin, and then Christ provided direct assurance of forgiveness when he told Peter to feed his lambs and sheep. Peter did such feeding on Pentecost and for years after that. He knew how to talk about forgiveness because he had been forgiven. Jesus' message to Peter was not a generalized description of law and gospel. The message was meant just for him.

One of the best examples of this kind of direct confrontation with the law and gospel came when Nathan, the prophet of the king of Israel, told David, "You are the man." That was the law. The Lord also put away David's sin, and he would not die as he deserved. That was the gospel. The message was meant just for David. Psalm 32 and Psalm 51 show that David understood both the law and gospel personally.

Christians are equipped to bring both the law and gospel to the world. Preaching law and gospel is not an academic theology lesson. God expects Christians to use all the equipment he has given to confront people with their personal sin so the gospel can be used to introduce them or reintroduce them to their personal Savior. Whether we are preaching to many or talking to one, we

3

must talk to people, not over them, around them or beneath them. We strive for that in our preaching and we can strive for the same thing in our counseling. Only when we talk to others can we give the relief Christ provides. That relief of heart, conscience and mind is what we mean by gospel resolution.

Three thousand on Pentecost learned that Christ paid for their sins. That news relieved their consciences when God worked the faith to believe the message. The gospel resolved their guilt problem. Jesus wanted the disciples to communicate the gospel and they did. God worked the faith. Peter himself was an example of gospel resolution because, when Jesus finished talking to him, Peter knew and believed that Jesus had been to the cross to pay for his sin. David was an example of gospel resolution because when Nathan told him God had put away his sin and he would not die, he knew he was a forgiven sinner. The weight of guilt was gone.

We have a completed gospel of forgiveness to share, and everyone needs to know personally that Christ's forgiveness is complete. That complete assurance of forgiveness is gospel resolution. Confronting sin puts us on the way to gospel resolution. When a person knows he or she needs the Savior, that's progress. Gospel resolution occurs when a person knows and believes *his* or *her* sins have been paid for in full by Jesus Christ. No one can make another person believe that. Only God can accomplish such a miracle. Our small but essential part is to do all we can to confront sin and communicate the gospel directly the way Jesus did, the way Peter did, the way Nathan did and the way thousands of Christ's disciples have communicated the gospel over the centuries. The results belong to God.

To illustrate the point, a man, Mr. Blakely, came reluctantly to talk to his pastor. His wife wanted him to come because she was concerned about his drinking. Every night he would drink a six-pack of beer. On the weekends he consumed much more. Mr. Blakely didn't think he had a problem. He didn't get violent; he tried to be a good father. He just needed to relax, and the beer helped him do that. Nevertheless, his wife was still concerned. The couple was drifting farther apart each day. She couldn't talk to him anymore. He couldn't stand her nagging. John Blakely had also been arrested for driving under the influence of alcohol, but he got off easy. That didn't help him confront his problem.

What would the pastor, Pastor James, do in a situation like that? Obviously John's drinking created a problem. Was drinking the only problem? Pastor James could simply talk to John about the sin of drunkenness, but his member wouldn't admit to being a drunk or an alcoholic. He could encourage John to go to a substance abuse center for an evaluation, hoping the people there could convince him he was an alcoholic. But even if he were convinced and decided to enter a program of rehabilitation, would that mean he would have to confront his sin? Was there another sin behind the sin of alcoholism? Would that sin be addressed? Would Pastor James' work be done? Where should he start? When would it end?

Some simple questions helped to uncover the sin behind the sin of drinking too much. For example, how long had John Blakely been drinking like this? When did it start to become a problem? What else was going on in John's life at the time? Why did Mrs. Blakely think the problem was worse now than it had been before? Was she objective in her evaluation?

The fact was that John began to drink much more heavily two-and-a-half years earlier. Before that his wife didn't even think he liked beer. The change was dramatic. Pastor James gained some helpful information, but it was not enough to resolve the problem yet. It was getting more difficult for Pastor James and Mr. Blakely to talk to each other. Most of the contact was through his wife. She was still concerned because nothing was getting better.

Finally she remembered that John started drinking about the same time his mother died. Mrs. Blakely didn't think the two had been unusually close as mother and son, so she didn't think her death could be part of the problem. The next time Pastor James met with John he asked about the death of his mother. John was sure he had grieved for her in a normal way and he didn't see any relationship between that and his drinking. He still couldn't see a problem.

Pastor James had an opportunity to ask a few more questions. What had the relationship with his mother been like? Although he didn't say it directly, the indications were that John had always been dominated by his mother. She tried to run his life when he was a child and didn't stop trying to run his life when he was an adult. She always had something to say about his job, his marriage, his children and him. Most of it wasn't very complimentary. Pastor James knew he was getting closer to the root of the problem.

The drinking was just a cover-up for the fact that John never really forgave his mother for the way she treated him. On top of everything else, Mrs. Blakely's constant nagging about his drinking was just like what his mother had always done. John thought he was free of his mother, but he was still a slave. He thought he was a slave to his wife, but the slavery was really taking the form of alcoholism.

The sin behind the sin in Mr. Blakely's life was a refusal to forgive. He was angry with his mother. Mrs. Blakely usually got the brunt of his anger, but John was really still angry with his mother.

That left Pastor James with a difficult problem. What could he do to help Mr. Blakely get rid of the anger he was feeling? How could he help someone forgive another when the other was dead? He couldn't tell John to go and talk to his mother. She had died almost three years earlier. Drinking was becoming a serious problem, but it wasn't the only problem. John had to deal with his alcoholism, but, more important, he had to face the reason why he was drinking. Pastor James knew what the problem was, and he knew that very few if any substance abuse centers could help John with the real problem. But he could. He was equipped with the gospel. He was equipped to deal with guilt and forgiveness. The substance abuse center would concentrate on alcohol rehabilitation.

Pastor James confronted John Blakely with his refusal to forgive. It didn't matter whether he was refusing to forgive his mother or his wife. The real problem was that John was refusing to forgive. He knew he should be forgiving, but he wouldn't do it. He decided to try to resolve the conflict he felt by drinking more. It wasn't helping, it was only making matters worse. Pastor James had to teach John to forgive. He had to teach the lesson so well that John would be equipped to forgive someone who was dead.

Pastor James could have been content to say, "John, you know you need to be forgiving. Jesus forgave you and he expects the same from you." He didn't do that. That was law and John needed the gospel to understand his own forgiveness. So, in a spiritual sense, he took John by the hand and walked with him all the way to the cross of the Lord Jesus. He showed John what Jesus did there. He wasn't just dying on the cross, Jesus was paying for John's refusal to forgive. He was paying for the forgiveness Pastor James was giving John. John, in turn, had the necessary forgiveness that could wipe the slate clean between his mother and himself. He could forgive her even though she was dead. That was the only way John's sin could be taken away. When John understood Christ's forgiveness, the conflict was resolved.

Pastor James helped John see the sin behind the sin of drinking. All of it was paid for there at the cross. Jesus took it all away by paying for it with his life. He helped John resolve both his refusal to forgive and his drinking. John saw that his drinking was the route he chose to take, not the route that would resolve his conflict and give him the peace he wanted and needed. His drinking was not only taking him farther away from his family, it was taking him farther away from God, who was the only one who could resolve the issue. John had more at stake than his marriage, his health, his job, his safety and the safety of others. He was in danger of leaving his Lord for good. He was trying to find peace in a bottle, but only God could give him the peace he needed and wanted.

Gospel resolution begins with finding sin and confronting it, applying the gospel and leaving the rest up to God. John didn't need to drink anymore. He found his peace in Christ. The rehabilitation program could deal with the addiction because John had confronted and resolved the conflict that caused it. John learned that refusing to forgive is a sin that produces internal conflict. Deadening the pain internal conflict causes is not sufficient to provide lasting peace, and it can do serious physical and spiritual damage.

Pastor James was well-equipped to do this work because he knew what guilt was and what to do with it. He was equipped with the law and gospel. A counselor who is not equipped with the law and gospel may be able to uncover guilt, but the best he can do is try to convince his client that he or she shouldn't be feeling guilty in the first place. As a result, no resolution occurs. If a Christian who is equipped with the law and gospel does not take the time, expend the effort or see the need to look for the sin behind the sin, no resolution occurs either, because he hasn't really dealt with the problem. If a Christian equipped with the law and gospel merely speaks the law and gospel at the people who seek his assistance, people will probably get the impression that he has a tape recorded generic message for all the people he talks to.

The lady who was brought to Jesus after she had been caught in the act of adultery didn't hear Jesus say, "I don't condemn," she heard him say, "I don't condemn *you*." The Jewish leaders who brought her to Jesus didn't hear him say, "I don't condemn," they heard him say, "If *you* are guiltless, go ahead and stone her." Jesus had individualized messages for her and for them. The woman needed and wanted forgiveness, the others didn't. The sins of the woman were resolved, taken away, gone because her forgiving Savior took them away. The pride and self-righteousness of the others kept them from receiving forgiveness. Jesus was talking to all the people directly about their own particular sin problems.

Sin is sin no matter what commandment is involved and no matter who commits the sin. The law addresses that. Likewise, forgiveness is forgiveness. The only forgiveness we have to offer is the complete forgiveness Jesus won for every sin. Gospel resolution occurs only when the guilt of specific sins is washed away by the forgiveness Jesus won. That way we are not just saying, "All sins have been forgiven," we're saying, "Your sins have been forgiven. That sin has been paid for."

Gospel resolution means that a sinner knows and believes he or she has full and free forgiveness. We cannot communicate that forgiveness by talking in generalities, either in the pulpit or in the counseling office. Like Jesus, like the apostles on Pentecost, like Nathan, we need to teach individuals to observe all the things Christ has taught us. He lived, died and rose again to obtain forgiveness, life and salvation that is ours to offer. These are historical facts, but we should not be content to give a generic message that is intended to address everyone but really addresses no one in particular.

Gospel resolution means a sinner knows that by God's judgment and declaration, his record of sins stands at zero. The fine has been paid and the receipt has been delivered into our hands. Jesus paid for everything we and everyone else have ever done wrong, especially the sins in one's heart and mind. Either the gospel resolves it, or people will continue to seek some alternative, temporary, unreliable resolution.

CHAPTER TWO
THE MINISTER'S RESPONSIBILITY TO SEEK RESOLUTION

A favorite biblical picture of God's relationship with his people is that of the shepherd with his sheep. The familiar words of Psalm 23 are probably the main reason people identify with this picture. It often prompts people to think of serene pastoral settings, quiet places set apart, safe and peaceful.

Actually the picture of the shepherd and his sheep goes much deeper as God presents it throughout his inspired word. To the undershepherds of Christ the picture has particular significance. God requires undershepherds, his ministers, to help, direct and provide for his people. Undershepherds have the word of God to give the sheep, the people who belong to Christ, God's people. And God provides guidance for his undershepherds. Many passages help us understand their responsibilities.

The Shepherd of Israel in the theocracy of God's chosen people was God himself. He provided the nurture, the direction, the discipline as their Shepherd. Later the people of Israel decided they wanted a king like all the other nations. They wanted a different shepherd. Consequently, the kings of Israel and Judah were responsible to God as undershepherds whether they acted well on that responsibility or not. A brief look at three of Israel's kings will illustrate the point.

Saul, the first king of Israel, serves as an example of a failure to carry out his responsibility as undershepherd, by either overstepping his limitations or neglecting his work. On most occasions in the latter part of his reign, Saul didn't realize he was supposed to be a shepherd and not just a warrior and leader for God's people. He ignored God's directions to be an undershepherd. In his pride he thought his kingship was his own to control as he saw fit to enhance his own position. As a result, both he and God's people suffered spiritually.

King David, on the other hand, provides a model for undershepherds to follow even though he had his own personal failings, weaknesses and sins to deal with. God led him (shepherded him), and consequently nothing he did was more important than teaching Israel to depend on God as the ultimate shepherd. Once David's reign was complete, all who held the position of king in Israel after him saw by example that God expected his kings to be shepherds with a primary concern for the spiritual welfare of the people who belonged to God.

King Solomon not only realized in the early years of his reign that he was to be the spiritual leader and shepherd of God's people, but he and his people witnessed the blessings God can and does pour out on his people when the rod and the staff of God's word are properly used to keep the sheep close to their shepherd. Solomon's prayer for wisdom and his prayer at the dedication of the temple of God indicate that his priority was the spiritual welfare of the people of God. He willingly accepted the responsibility to be an undershepherd for God. Once again, however, pride eventually entered the picture and created problems.

In spite of the human frailties of both King David and King Solomon, these men understood that their primary responsibility was to shepherd God's people by caring for their spiritual needs. We can say this without ignoring their sins or their own need for shepherding by God. Every king who followed them should have recognized the same truth. Unfortunately, most of them did not.

The books of Kings and Chronicles don't say that the kings didn't shepherd God's people. They certainly did. All the kings had a direct influence on the spiritual lives of the people of God. The problem was that most of that influence led God's people away from God. The kings of Israel and Judah, for the most part, ignored their responsibility to shepherd God's people *the way God wanted them to be shepherded.* They turned the worship of the people away from God to other gods. They led them to trust that idols could provide blessings which, in fact, only the Triune God could give.

This intentionally oversimplified illustration teaches a great many lessons for us who are kings and priests in our own right through Jesus' work. In addition we have a ministry by virtue of our call to serve other kings and queens, priests and priestesses of God. We and they are all sheep who need God's shepherding, if we are to have the blessings Christ won and God wants us to have.

We do not have the right to decide what form our ministry is to take, the way Saul thought he did. God decides that. The authority belongs to God. Our work is to shepherd God's people on behalf of the one who owns them. The temptation may be great, as it was for Saul, to think we have better qualities or resources than God to decide what his people need. Nevertheless, all the gifts, talents, energies and ideas God gives are doomed to the

13

same miserable failure Saul experienced if we forget, as he did, that we are totally dependent on God.

Like David and Solomon we are shepherds, spiritual leaders for God's people. Our primary responsibility is the people's spiritual welfare *as God directs it*. We can only carry out that responsibility by leading the people with the word of God. At the same time, we need the same shepherding God wants for the rest of his people. We need forgiveness, direction from God's word, the law to show us our sins and the gospel to assure us of forgiveness, just as much as the people we shepherd. We need growth in God's word, or soon we will have nothing to give. Pastors and teachers can run dry or starve spiritually because their own relationship with God is dying of thirst and hunger for his word. That does not happen because God hasn't provided for us. It is the result of neglect or refusal to eat of the bread of life. This danger exists for all of God's people, including undershepherds.

We should be able to understand the warnings to be gathered from the example of the vast majority of the remaining kings of Israel and Judah. The people of Israel looked to them as spiritual leaders. They led the people spiritually. The problem was that their shepherding was not the kind of shepherding God wanted his people to have. Almost to a man, they turned elsewhere for nurture, direction, provision and other blessings when in reality only God could provide them. No wonder most of them had nothing of value to give God's people. No wonder the people found no blessing. They were looking in all the wrong places.

Similarly we have an abundance of deceptive alternative sources to use to give comfort to the people of God. Bookshelves and media marts are filled with proposed alternatives to the word of God. But is this shepherding as God directs us to shepherd his people?

Only his word can measure that. Too often the available material is not tested at all against the standard of the word of God. If it were, much of it would fail the test the way the kings of the divided kingdom failed because they didn't direct God's people the way God wanted them to be directed.

We must also examine ourselves by the same standard. Christ's undershepherds are unalterably dedicated to the word of God as God's only source of peace and hope. We hold church services weekly and more just because we know our people have spiritual needs, which we must continually help satisfy with the word of God. But we can do more than offer corporate worship to satisfy those needs, can't we? Anyone can turn to the radio or television and find some kind of religious satisfaction. Addressing special personal problems is made as simple as buying a book or a tape in a Christian bookstore even though the material may not share our scriptural foundation. In short, we have the best and only real answer to the world's needs, but others may be doing far more with much less to address those needs.

Warnings and disclaimers about material from heterodox writers are not worth much if we are content to say, "This isn't sound scriptural material, but it might give you something to think about. It might help you with some of the problems you're having. It might help you work out your problems." The only implication a statement like that can make is that people who don't have a firm foundation in the law and gospel know and care more about coping with human problems than biblical Christians do.

Many forms of media and agencies bear the name "Christian" whether they actually live up to the genuine qualities of Christianity or not. Most pastors would not be particularly happy to hear their people say they don't need to come to church because they have television and radio ministries to serve them. That's not church and that's not shepherding, to say nothing of the dubious quality of the message they may be hearing. Should we be any more satisfied to know that our people are finding some spiritual satisfaction for their individual needs elsewhere? God's word is being taught in its truth and purity in the church as a sanctuary for God's people. We are responsible for shepherding them one at a time or corporately to the one true God, not to other gods that aren't gods at all and not to another gospel that is really no gospel at all (cf. Galatians 1).

Add to all this that the *Yellow Pages* are literally filled with agencies to provide help for almost anything, and the problem only increases. Our people have dozens of hotlines to call for answers to their personal, physical and emotional needs. Few of them propose to deal with the spiritual side of the problem. For example, Alcoholics Anonymous may have helped a great many people recover from alcoholism. AA does not, however, intend to be a religion, unless we let it become the religion of the people we serve. Too often the resulting religion is either Phariseeism or despair because no one identifies, "the being greater than the alcoholic" that AA promotes.

On another front, psychologists and psychiatrists have advanced numerous theories and psychotherapies in the last fifty years. The whole subject has become popularized with magazines like *Psychology Today*. Psychotherapies like Janov's "Primal Scream," Transactional Analysis, Cognitive Therapy and many others have been described in books and articles for general audiences. They often imply that people can solve their own problems when they read the humanistic step-by-step, easy-to-follow instructions. Once again the problem is the impression that almost everyone else is more interested in and capable of helping people work out their problems than the church is. Most of this material doesn't even pretend to be Christian, it only pretends to help. Who are the gods? Where are the shepherds? What kind of help is this?

It doesn't take long for a busy pastor to prepare for his Bible class if he just turns on a video or audio tape and sits back to listen or watch with his people. It's easy to counsel a depressed or anxious person by taking a book off the shelf and giving it to a troubled person to read. Pastors will have a great deal of time for other things as long as counseling work consists of referring troubled people somewhere else. But is that shepherding?

The Old Testament urges us to think about our responsibility as undershepherds. John 10 summarizes the work of the ultimate Shepherd, Jesus Christ. In that chapter Jesus brings out several essential points. First, the sheep belong to Jesus; second, Jesus was willing to die for the sheep; third, Jesus' life, death and resurrection saved the sheep; fourth, only Jesus can give his sheep the blessings they need to live and die as he wills; fifth, Jesus has entrusted us with the responsibility of spreading this news among his sheep.

The sheep belong to Jesus. He contrasts himself with those who are merely hired to tend the sheep. He owns them because he paid for them with his life. No one can equal the concern he has for those who belong to him, not even those who work in his name. We serve Jesus as ministers because we ourselves belong to him and because we have the privilege of working in his behalf. The sheep belong to him. Our work is merely to present Jesus' concern to the sheep. He is the one of a kind Good Shepherd, so we have a one of a kind vocation.

Jesus was willing and able to die for his sheep because he loved them enough to complete the work of redemption to save their lives. In addition he had the power

17

to lay down his life and the power to take it again. He was made to be sin, yet he knew no sin. He became the substitute sinner to bear sinners' punishment and to die their death vicariously. Only the Good Shepherd could do that. Any shepherd might die trying to save the life of a sheep, but then both the shepherd and the sheep would probably die. That was not the case with the Good Shepherd. His life was an acceptable *sacrifice for* the people of the world. He won by dying and rising again. Only Jesus has that kind of power.

Jesus' death was intimately connected with his resurrection. Jesus has the power of life in his hands, life on earth and life in heaven. Life as Jesus speaks about it, real life, includes a life worth living and a death worth dying. In life and death Jesus' sheep are safe with him. He is the Good Shepherd.

Jesus expressed his concern for gathering sheep together. He is concerned about sheep that are not yet his through faith. Whether he shows his concern for many at once or each one individually, he is the only real hope the sheep have. Either way, Jesus is the Good Shepherd. His life, his death and his resurrection save sheep, sheep that aren't yet in his fold and sheep that are. That is the essential message the word of God proclaims and the essential message of the faithful undershepherd.

St. Paul told the Corinthians that when he was with them he never claimed to know anything except Jesus Christ, crucified and risen from death. St. Paul knew he was nothing more and nothing less than an undershepherd of the only Shepherd. All he had to offer was the news about the Shepherd who laid down his life for the sheep. Nothing else mattered. Nothing else matters and nothing else saves people now either.

No one can add anything to the Good Shepherd's completed work of salvation, and nothing can duplicate it. As undershepherds in the same privileged position as Paul and all the apostles, we have nothing that can help people more than the word of God that presents Jesus' finished work. Furthermore, we have the responsibility to give his sheep everything Jesus wants them to have, everything he won for them, whether or not it happens to be currently popular. That is the essence of Christ's Great Commission.

The question that remains for us is how to give Jesus' sheep everything he won. In our church circles we don't have a problem realizing the need for Christ's people to gather to hear his word. Most pastors and teachers continually encourage regular use of the means of grace with other believers. On the other hand, we can't forget that the same Good Shepherd was concerned enough about one endangered sheep to advise leaving ninety-nine alone to meet the special needs of one. Both the individual and the ninety-nine need to know the Good Shepherd better. The only difference between the one and the ninety-nine is the particular method of communicating the significance of Christ's life, death and resurrection.

Most of us would admit that we have considerable room to improve our skills, whether ministering to many or to one. We should also recognize that the concern for the individual deserves at least as much attention as our concern for the corporate church. The Apostle Paul recognized that he was a debtor to everyone. He owed the gospel to others because Christ had given it to him. Paul was forgiven by the gospel, and he was equipped with it. So are we. What further skills do we need? How do those skills need to be honed? How inclined are we to feel incapable, too taxed, too ready to turn to a hired hand instead of shepherding on behalf of the Good Shepherd with news about the Good Shepherd? We can always get better at our work whatever form it takes. God knows how to provide the means to improve.

CHAPTER THREE
THE NECESSITY OF RESOLUTION

"Unresolved guilt" is a fairly common psychological term. It generally means that some guilt in a person's past is continuing to produce problems in the present. Gospel resolution occurs when a person realizes that *all his guilt has been resolved.* God has given us the means of grace for creating and maintaining confidence that Christ has resolved all guilt. He paid for all sin in general and each sin in particular.

God intends people to know and believe that fact. For that reason alone, gospel resolution is a necessity. God's gift of full and free forgiveness produces the peace God wants his people to have. Nevertheless, many people don't realize God's peace is theirs because something is standing in the way of it. We can help people find out what is standing in the way of experiencing resolution of their guilt by using both the law and gospel God has entrusted to us.

Too often pastors and teachers may give prepackaged answers to personal problems people have without first listening to a thorough presentation of the problems. We can liken treating an emotional problem to solving an algebra problem. In algebra you may already know the answer. But you must also establish the process for obtaining the answer before your work is done. The same is true of gospel resolution.

In dealing with personal problems we may already know what the answer is and then fail to assemble a process for arriving at the answer. We know, for example, that real peace is only produced by the gospel. Why not just give a troubled person the gospel and let it go at that? Our people not only need the law and gospel, they also need to understand what the law and gospel say to them personally.

A patient would justifiably be dissatisfied hearing the doctor diagnose his problem as an illness. He would probably want to know what kind of illness it is and what can be done about it. In the same way, a troubled Christian would have good reason to be dissatisfied if a pastor tells him that the reason for his lack of peace is sin, without examining what the sin is and what can be, or better, has been done about it.

Take the case of Connie, for example, who was suffering with a mild to moderate form of paranoia. She was extremely anxious. She was convinced other people were talking behind her back, avoiding her and purposely trying to hurt her. She believed someone was always watching her house. Her paranoia became an obsession. She was upsetting her own household and the households of relatives and neighbors. Her marriage was severely stressed.

I first learned about Connie's problem by referral in a meeting with her extended family. The purpose of the meeting was to discuss ways to help Connie and those concerned about her to handle her problem. The general consensus was that Connie probably needed psychiatric help, at least to reduce her anxiety. Perhaps medication would be appropriate in a psychiatrist's judgment. We also looked for a way to provide spiritual care, because everyone, including Connie, agreed that she needed God's help.

Connie met with a psychiatrist, who prescribed medication to reduce her anxiety. The anxiety subsided, but the paranoia continued. Rather than feeling more relaxed, she simply felt more tired. She began to sleep more, but her sleep was restless. Her psychiatrist tried to convince Connie that her feelings had no basis in reality, but that only raised more suspicions and aggravated the problem. She became more convinced than ever that the events she described were really happening.

I first met Connie personally at her home, because by this time she almost never left home. She was extremely agitated. I urged her to take the medication her doctor had prescribed and to contact him again. She agreed. In addition she agreed to meet with me at my church office. Connie needed to get out of the house whether she liked it or not. She was very cooperative. Connie was one of the most punctual and faithful counselees I have ever had the privilege to work with. She never missed an appointment and she was never late. Obviously she wanted to get rid of her paranoia. We met for an hour a week for about six weeks.

The purpose of the first meeting was to establish confidence between Connie and me. This was an important meeting because of Connie's paranoid condition. Since her family and her psychiatrist had not succeeded in convincing Connie that her paranoid feelings were unfounded, I decided to listen to what Connie thought others around her were doing without questioning the reality of her perceptions. Within thirty minutes she was saying, "I'm not sure whether this really happened or not, but. . . ." She was giving indications that she doubted her own paranoid feelings. By the end of the first session her anxiety had diminished considerably.

We enlisted the cooperation and support of those closest to her. She agreed that she would tell her husband and other supporters what we had talked about in our sessions and then her husband would call to tell me what he understood her to be saying. The reports were always accurate representations of what had taken place. By the second meeting Connie's paranoia had diminished considerably. She began to give indications that her paranoia was really covering something else. Connie felt extremely guilty. The guilt she felt was real, even if the paranoid feelings weren't based on real situations. Neither Connie nor I knew how much we could do about the paranoia, but we knew that with God's help she could become "the most spiritually healthy paranoid in town."

By the third meeting, no paranoid feelings remained. She also had no ambition. She contacted her doctor again to determine whether he could reduce her medication or change it. With a change in medication she had a little more energy. She began to talk about the guilt she was feeling. The medication was not resolving the problem of her guilt, it was merely reducing the anxiety she had been experiencing. Connie felt trapped. With less paranoia she felt more guilty. The guilt only diminished when anxious paranoia took its place. She thought the best she could hope for was to learn to cope better with these alternating problems.

This third session became the most important session of all. I asked what Connie thought God could do to help her. She spent about fifteen minutes talking about the ways God promised to help people carry their burdens. She believed she would be able to cope with God's help. I told Connie I didn't believe the Bible gives us any reason to believe that God would *help* her carry her guilt. That shocked her. She had always been taught that God would help her in her time of need. I told her I believed that too, but I didn't believe that meant God would help her carry her guilt. She was curious about that.

I suggested that Connie open the Bible on the desk and read Matthew 11:28-29: "Come to me, all you who are weary and burdened, and I will give you rest. Take my yoke upon you and learn from me, for I am gentle and humble in heart, and you will find rest for your souls."

After she read the passage I asked her what God meant by "rest." She thought for a few more minutes and said, "God wants me to put it down. He wants me to dump it." God didn't promise to help her carry her burdens, he wanted to *carry them for her.* God wanted her to dump them all at the cross. That became the key word. She wrote, "Just dump it" on a piece of paper and taped it to her refrigerator. Her husband used her words whenever she began to appear anxious. God wanted her to "dump it."

The cross was the place to leave the guilt and anxiety. We took what I have come to call a walk to Calvary. Connie saw her sins vividly and she could also see her Savior vividly. He was dying to give her rest. That fact became a reality for Connie. She could dump her sins because she knew where to go with them and that they had been paid for. The guilt was gone, resolved. Under the doctor's supervision she slowly withdrew from her medication. She no longer needed it to cope with her problem. Only the cross of Christ could resolve her guilt and bring her account to zero, not only on God's records, but in her own mind.

Connie had been punishing herself to the point of mental illness instead of resolving the real problem that was behind it all. When God accomplished the resolution, the results were astonishing. The paranoia and the anxiety were gone. Along with them, the family disturbances, the marriage problems and the baby-sitting of this adult were all gone too. She worked hard to accomplish that, she cooperated fully, but God performed the miracle.

An adolescent, Carl, had been closely associated with a tragedy that might traumatize anyone. His closest friends were killed by their father, who also killed their mother and then himself. Carl's parents, faithful church members, were naturally concerned about the impact all this would have on their son. Surprisingly, he seemed to handle the situation much better than his parents had hoped. We discussed possible problems to watch for, but none of them seemed to occur.

As time went on, however, Carl became more attached to his father and more uneasy when he was gone. His parents did the best they could to give their son as much attention, Christian love and support as possible. Things seemed to improve. It was possible that the apparent upset in the child's life was caused by a change in his father's work schedule, but we did not ignore the previous tragedy as a possible contributing factor. It just didn't seem to be the primary problem.

Matters grew worse over the next few months. Almost every night Carl would come to his parents' room to sleep with them, but usually he couldn't remember going to their room. Carl began to have nightmares. He could not remember what they were about. When he did awaken he only knew he was frightened. The nightmares turned to night terrors. Almost nightly he would run screaming, sweating, shaking and running unconsciously through the house, but Carl couldn't remember anything. Over the course of a month these night terrors occurred four to six times a week, usually lasting about twenty minutes.

Carl's parents asked if he would be willing to talk to me. He was more than willing. In consultation about the problem we agreed that I would talk to Carl and that we would stay in close contact to determine the best steps to take. Invaluable medical assistance and advice was available. Psychological assistance and testing was available. Even psychiatric consultation was available, if necessary. All this could be done, if necessary, and we could still deal directly with the spiritual needs the child had.

Once again, the first session was spent in gaining Carl's confidence. That wasn't hard. Carl couldn't spend the night with friends because he was afraid he would have a night terror his friends and their parents wouldn't understand. He didn't like what was happening and he didn't understand it. His parents were very patient and concerned, but they felt helpless. Carl said he was willing to do whatever he had to do so he wouldn't have these screaming night terrors again, but he could not remember when he had his first dream nor could he remember what any of the dreams were about. His assignment was to keep track of how many times he awoke during the week, to wake from his sleep and try to remember what he had been dreaming. His parents even tape recorded two of the events and he listened to them. He was hardly able to believe what he was hearing. I could hardly believe it either. Carl's parents had been living with a nightmare of their own.

One week later Carl brought the tape and the report that he could not remember any of the recent dreams but he did remember one from about three-and-a-half years earlier. The dream of three-and-a-half years earlier was so vivid that Carl could remember the color of the eyes of the people in it. The following week Carl had no dreams.

The next week Carl reported that he could remember some of the dreams he had more recently. All the dreams he reported involved different settings, but the plot was always the same as the first one. We took note of that together, and Carl realized that his dreams were very predictable. Even though the scenes changed, the plot was always the same. Carl had one night terror the following week. When he awoke he could remember the dream. Once again the plot was the same.

We examined what else was happening in Carl's life at the time he had the first nightmare three-and-a-half years earlier. He could not remember any particularly significant events. His parents and I knew the time corresponded with the murder of his friends. We suspected Carl was still feeling threatened by the event. The problem was how to get Carl to realize it. Carl was trying to remember, but he couldn't.

"Did anything happen at school three-and-a-half years ago?" He remembered that his grades went down a little. "What else happened about that time?" Carl came up with a few more things completely unrelated to the murder. "How were you getting along with your friends at that time?" Then it came out. That was when his friends died. "How did that make you feel?" Carl's answer astounded me. He said, "They probably would have died anyway." Carl's answer didn't fit the assumption his parents and I had made. He didn't say he could have been killed if he had been with them. He had, in fact, planned to spend the night with the children, but he couldn't go because he was sick. But "they probably would have died anyway." Carl had never been afraid that he would be a victim. In his heart he believed that his presence with them that night could have saved their lives. He felt guilt, not fear. He rationalized his guilt to deal with it.

Carl had completely suppressed his guilt into his subconscious, where the conflict could only escape through his night terrors. The plot of his dreams was an accurate representation of his own subconscious feelings. He was a bystander, but he believed he was responsible and should be punished, so the people in his dreams chased him to punish him. But in his dreams no one caught him. Carl never did receive the punishment he thought he deserved from anyone else. His own subconscious was taking care of that.

Bringing the suppressed guilt of three-and-a-half years to consciousness was more than a little frightening for everyone involved. His parents and I talked about possible reactions to this trauma. Once again we were prepared with medical, psychological and psychiatric personnel if they were needed. His parents understood that he could have more night terrors from habit or from the trauma he experienced as he recreated the events. None of that took place. Carl never had another night terror.

Carl realized that he had been rationalizing the guilt he felt, but he had not resolved it. That is a difficult job for anyone, especially an adolescent. Like Connie, this boy and I went hand in hand to the cross of Jesus. Carl knew he couldn't do anything about what had happened, but he knew Jesus could take away all the guilt he felt. He gave some of the most beautiful expressions of Christian faith a pastor could hope to hear from any of his members, youth and adult alike.

Both of these examples show that nothing but complete resolution can really do away with a guilt-based emotional problem a person is experiencing. Medication can cover it. Rationalization can suppress it. Only Christ can resolve it by his work of atonement. Connie's paranoia stopped because she had no more need to cover her guilt with it. Carl's night terrors stopped because the subconscious conflict had been resolved. The spiritual life of these people is much more complete than they ever experienced before. They are ready for heaven, the main goal of the peace Jesus gives. But for right now, they are people at peace with God and themselves because of what Jesus did two thousand years ago. Their sins, real or imagined, are resolved.

While these examples illustrate the necessity of resolution, failure to reach resolution might illustrate its importance even better. The previous examples have shown the relationship often existing between underlying guilt and emotional problems. The presenting problem was only the tip of the iceberg. We can easily be content to deal with one-eighth of the problem above the surface while ignoring the seven-eighths below. Alcoholism and drug abuse offer some prime examples of dealing with the problem of substance abuse without addressing the underlying cause.

Bill, for example, had been an alcoholic and a drug abuser since he was sixteen. By the time he was twenty-five he drank forty cans of beer and used $100 worth of cocaine daily. He could not hold a job for more than two weeks. He played with a band in bars and nightclubs, making it possible for him to support his habits, but the band broke up. No one could talk to him about his problem until he found himself in a different part of the country without knowing how he got there. That frightened him enough to do something about it.

Bill was ready to confront the problem. Ground rules were important. We had a set time to meet and no excuses were acceptable for failure to come. For four days we met intensively for at least an hour to arrive at the underlying problem as soon as possible. Bill's parents were closely involved.

Bill was an atypical alcoholic, and normal treatment programs were not appropriate. He had to do his work on his own together with his support group, which included his parents and me. We also had the benefit of a substance abuse expert and a medical doctor. They confirmed that

Bill was atypical, particularly because he was alive after such tremendous consumption of alcohol and drugs. Surprisingly he had very few side effects.

Bill had a great many fears to conquer. He had not held a regular job for years. The years between 16 and 25 were almost a blank. The normal maturing process had been stunted. In short, Bill was a sixteen-year-old in a twenty-five-year-old body. He grew to trust his closest supporters, but he still carried a great deal of guilt about what he had done before and during this dark period of his life. He studied diligently to try to understand God's message to him in the law and gospel, but he used negative experiences with the church as an excuse for rejecting God's forgiveness. Bill couldn't see himself as forgiven and so the church, to him, meant condemnation, not forgiveness. He considered everyone who encouraged him to attend church a fanatic. He was so fanatically anti-church that he exceeded the fanaticism of the people he accused.

Bill and I had one of the most open and honest relationships of anyone I have ever counseled. We both respected each other, and our sessions were frank. But respect was not enough to overcome Bill's resentment or the depression he was beginning to experience. The loss of the alcohol and drugs in his life was a major loss that produced what is sometimes called "a dry drunk depression." He had been off drugs for over six months. He was holding a steady job and making good money. He was surprising people all over town by repaying long-standing debts. Everything was going fine except that Bill was still depressed and wanted nothing to do with God.

Bill may never drink again in his life. He may continue to be successful in his work and upstanding in his responsibilities. He may continue to be a good friend with a great deal of respect and love for those who helped him, but all of us know the work isn't done yet. Bill still refuses to accept that God has been and still wants to be an integral part of his life. At this point we have to be content that the law and gospel were both delivered. God did not promise they would have the effect we want when we want it. Obviously God is not finished with his work either, because the door is still open, and Bill is still alive in his time of grace. We still pray for a serious change in heart and mind along with his continued sobriety.

In almost any area of counseling, an end of paranoia, night terrors or substance abuse would be enough for the counselor to expect. Where God is concerned, however, these are only beginnings. The work of the pastor as counselor in his office is much like the work of the pastor as a counselor for the dying and those close to them. When the doctor's work ends, in a sense, the pastor's work begins. Resolution of the problem takes place when a person knows the peace of mind and heart the gospel gives, and understands the importance of living in Christ. Without Christ, solving the superficial problem is of no eternal significance.

We are interested in changing more than the behavior of a troubled person. We are interested in repentance, a change of heart and mind, because that is what God wants even more than a change in behavior. In fact, from God's point of view, a change in heart and mind by the gospel is the only way to effect a genuine change of behavior.

Problems and serious illnesses, in some cases, may be God's way of getting people to do something about the deeper spiritual problems they have. Many ministers of the gospel have seen deathbed conversions that illustrate the point. How thankful we can be when a person hurts enough to do something about the pain before he reaches his deathbed. Often the problems linger, however. That does not mean God has forsaken the troubled person.

God may be saying, "Learn by this thorn in the flesh to trust me more and see your Savior's love more clearly."

Regardless of the avenues God uses, we need to be prepared with the answer God gives, "I love you and I know what I'm doing with you, dear child. Trust me."

The spiritual aspect of genuine Christian counseling is not always easy or even possible to measure. Changes in behavior are easy to measure. Either they occur or they don't. Behavioral changes can be tested and documented, and methods for obtaining them can be measured and evaluated. But only God knows what is in a person's heart. The measure he uses for determining our success or failure is not the same as the measure most counselors use. He simply tells us to use his word, law and gospel, and leave the rest up to him. That is faithfulness and success.

Faithfulness to our responsibilities to God and the people we serve may or may not solve their problems. Our people themselves may or may not *really want* to solve their problems. People may get better without showing evidence of the spiritual results we seek, concluding that they have no real need for God and his word. That is in God's hands. No one could carry the weight of this responsibility for God's people without understanding that we plant the word, and God makes it grow as he sees fit. Faithfulness to God's word makes gospel resolution both possible and necessary. We need to be ready to use it and to reject any lesser goals.

CHAPTER FOUR
THE LAW PREPARES
FOR RESOLUTION

One Sunday President Calvin Coolidge, a man of few words, returned from church, and his wife asked him what the minister talked about. The president said, "Sin." She asked what the minister had to say about sin. "He was agin' it," was the reply.

Everyone, Christian or not, should realize that God is "agin'" sin. But God is not vague where sin is concerned. He gave three different law codes to his Old Testament people. One directed their worship; another governed them; another established his holy definition of morality. All three of those codes defined sin whether it was directed against God or against another human being. God wanted his people to understand sin so he could prepare them for his answer to the sin problem, forgiveness won by Jesus Christ.

The moral law serves as a mirror to show us our sin. It serves as a curb to check coarse outbursts of sin. It also serves as a rule or guide for Christians who already know the love of their forgiving Savior, but look for the direction of the law to show them how to love God and others in a way that pleases him. All people need a concrete definition of what constitutes sin and what constitutes a God-pleasing life. All three purposes of the law have their place in personal counseling just as they do in Scriptural preaching. Only when people experience God's judgment on sin will they appreciate the importance of Christ's redemptive work.

The law is not a means of grace, it is a means to an end. The law is the handmaid of the gospel, intended to prepare the heart for planting the gospel seed. We might think the law is the last thing people need to hear when they come to our offices in tears and apparent hopelessness. Only listening to them present their problems will reveal whether they need to hear the law or the gospel at that time. We cannot assume that the law has already done its work just because a person is hurting. Sin causes the pain, not the law.

To illustrate the use of the law as a mirror, consider this. Diane came to my office as she had often come in the past to talk about the sad state of her marriage. Her husband had moved out months before. She had done everything she could to try to win him back. She had expressed her willingness to forgive him for the extramarital affair that broke the marriage bond, but nothing brought the two closer together. She could no longer tolerate the constant ups and downs, hoping and then doubting that the marriage problems could be resolved.

Often the first words a person speaks in a counseling session are the most important words in the session. In this case, Diane's first words were, "I feel so guilty." Then, as if she were a different person, she began to talk about all the things her husband was doing that made her angry. I told her I was confused. I could understand her anger and hopelessness, but she had said she felt guilty.

Diane felt guilty because of her anger with her husband. She knew a Christian shouldn't have those feelings. She didn't know what to do to get over them. Obviously Diane needed the gospel, but she also needed the law. I asked her to list the thoughts she had toward her husband. The list was quite long with good reason. I asked her what she intended to do with them. She answered that she just felt guilty. "So, you've decided to deal with those thoughts by feeling guilty. That is how you intend to justify feeling the way you do. You believe that you deserve to have these sinful thoughts if you feel guilty about them afterwards?"

Diane had not looked at her thoughts and feeling that way before. She had more than enough justification for anger, because her husband's actions were unquestionably sinful. But when Diane confronted her own sinfulness, the sin of trying to pay for her anger with her own guilt, she realized she was headed in the wrong spiritual direction. She was walking away from the cross, when only walking toward it would resolve her guilty feelings. She was trying to pay for her own sins with feelings of guilt.

When she saw her sin, she looked to God to resolve it. Christ's forgiveness equipped her to forgive her husband and she could also forgive herself. Christ earned forgiveness for both of them. She still shed tears, but they were not tears of guilt, they were tears of mourning over the loss of the marriage God had established. She also shed tears of joy because of the relief she experienced.

Forty to fifty percent of all marriages end in divorce. The need to apply the law to these situations is obvious to people who do much or little counseling. One more complex case exemplifies the use of the law as both a mirror and a curb, the way it applies to various aspects of marriage problems.

A young couple, the Hursts, were having serious problems in their marriage. Mrs. Hurst was drinking too much. At parties her flirtations became offensive. She blamed her behavior on her husband's increasing violence. He pushed her, threatened her and once even cracked a wall in their home by pushing her into it. After drinking too much at a party, Mrs. Hurst was seriously injured in a car accident that was her fault. Her stay in the hospital involved a long recovery from surgery. During my regular hospital visits with Mrs. Hurst, the problems with her husband began to surface, but she was afraid to do or say anything about them to him. She hoped he would be able to see what was happening to their marriage. She thought things would get better when he realized how serious her injuries were and how slow her recovery would be. She did not want to hear that her drinking might be contributing to the problems, or that her flirtations were unacceptable and dangerous for a young and attractive married woman.

Jane Hurst decided to handle matters her own way. When the violence increased even during her recovery period at home, she never told her husband, Matt, to stop—that she would not tolerate his abuse. Instead, without warning, she left home with her child and moved in with her mother. Her husband was furious. Jane and her mother believed Matt had serious mental problems.

Matt and Jane then consented to counsel with both me and a psychologist. They both agreed to psychological testing, if I was allowed to meet with them and the psychologist for the evaluations. Having secured the proper releases of information, Matt, Jane, the psychologist and I met to search for the root of the problem. Matt's violent behavior was unacceptable. Jane's drinking and flirtations added to the problem. Both had found unacceptable ways of demonstrating their dissatisfaction with each other. They both needed to stop their destructive behavior as they tried to solve their problems. The law as a curb helped accomplish some of that.

The underlying problem surfaced as frustration Matt was experiencing because he had to fight for Jane's attention and love. Jane responded by drinking and flirting with other men. Finally, the breaking point came when Jane left home and moved in with her mother. The bond that should have existed between husband and wife had been broken, and the bond between mother and daughter was reestablished. That increased Matt's frustration to the breaking point.

The law addressed Matt's violence and hostility toward his wife and his mother-in-law. It condemned Jane's substance abuse and flirtations. In addition, the law condemned Jane's departure from her husband to go to her mother's house, and it condemned her mother's interference. The problems were numerous and difficult. Matt wanted to be with his wife and children on his terms. Jane wanted to be out of the family home. Jane's mother never wanted to see Matt again.

The law defined all the sins and condemned them. The law, however, could not provide the motivation to accomplish resolution. A mere human cannot do what only God can accomplish. Likewise, the law cannot do what only the gospel can accomplish. The law can show people the loving thing to do, but only the gospel can provide the love the law demands.

How many times have you heard, "I want to do the loving thing. But how do I know what the loving thing is?" The law shows people what to do in love. The law was given by God not only to tell us when we haven't loved (mirror), or that we had better love (curb), but also to show us how to love.

Many of our people are familiar with the principles of "Tough Love." In simple terms, "Tough Love" means telling people they cannot get away with unacceptable behavior. "Tough Love" means laying down the law and attaching a price that must be paid for unacceptable actions. "Tough Love" is often used with delinquent children, substance abusers and others engaged in unacceptable behavior. It is a process based on common sense as much as anything else. Dr. James Dobson's *Love Must Be Tough* has also given it a "Christian" garb. He applies it to difficult marriage situations. This kind of love is tough both because it is difficult for people to show and difficult for people to accept. "Tough Love" is law and works apart from the gospel, if only to curb the sin.

Christians, however, can and will use "Tough Love" with a gospel motivation. Gospel motivated love will show in a way that will do another person the most good, even if it's "tough" to do. Only the gospel produces a Jesus-centered use of "Tough Love." God's "Tough Love" always asks, "Lord, what do you want me to do with Jesus' love for me and for this other person?" Too often people determine the loving thing to do by asking merely what will make them feel good, not what other people need and what Jesus would do.

Jane Hurst, who turned to drink and to her mother to resolve her marital problems, provided an example of what can happen when a person is led by feelings and fears instead of God's clear guidelines. Another young lady had a similar problem showing love properly. She was having problems getting along with her mother. Both the young lady and her husband were dominated by their own parents and their in-laws. Little, if anything, could be done to change the behavior of their parents. The problem was that the young lady and her husband were both inclined to accept the guilt trips their parents constantly placed on them. As a rule, for every person who knows how to put people on guilt trips, someone is available to take the trip. That was certainly true in this case.

The couple had to learn how to avoid taking guilt trips. They both felt they would be disobedient and disrespectful children if they didn't do what their parents wanted them to do. The more they tried to stand up to their parents, the worse things became for them.

The matter reached crisis proportions when Rachel tried to stand up to her mother's unreasonable expectations, only to have her mother collapse in her driveway. Rachel talked to her mother there in the driveway and told her she was sorry and would do what her mother wanted her to do. I asked how that made her feel. Rachel felt she had been manipulated into doing her mother's will again. She was right.

Rachel was determined to back off on her attempts to gain independence from her mother. What else could she do? She asked, "What would you do if your mother collapsed in your driveway?" I told Rachel that I would call the paramedics immediately so she could receive the medical attention she apparently needed.

Several days later Rachel called very excited and happy. Once again she had tried to stand up to her mother's unreasonable demands. Once again her mother collapsed in the driveway. This time Rachel left her immediately to call the paramedics. By the time the paramedics arrived, Rachel's mother was in the house drinking coffee with her daughter. She never tried that form of manipulation again. Rachel and her husband were encouraged to go on and find other ways to show their parents that manipulation did not accomplish the results they desired. The guilt trips weren't as easy to give or take anymore. Other more loving ways worked better.

In another situation several members of a family came with a concern about a sixty-five-year-old man named Tom. He was drinking far too much. To complicate the matter even more, Tom was a diabetic. The family didn't know how to confront Tom's alcoholism. Something had to be done because he was passing out on a regular basis when he was drinking. Everyone was afraid Tom would get angry, refuse to listen, leave or perhaps even commit suicide if anyone tried to confront him with his problem. Something had to be done, but what?

The family members decided that the best way to address the problem would be to get Tom to see a doctor who was aware of his drinking problem. The doctor could address it from a medical point of view.

Getting Tom to the doctor was no problem. He was concerned about his health too, but he blamed his poor physical condition on his diabetes. The doctor prescribed a number of tests to determine why Tom was passing out so often. His diabetes was not an isolated problem. It could have been controlled with a proper diet. The insulin was producing comas on a regular basis because it caused low blood sugar levels. The combination of hypoglycemia and drinking was deadly. A brain scan also showed that he was suffering from serious deterioration of the brain caused by drinking. That, in turn, contributed to other functional problems he was having. The whole situation was a vicious circle with drinking a deadly part of it. By that time Tom knew he was an alcoholic. The first step was past.

The family was again faced with some difficult decisions. They decided that constant companionship was the best way to help Tom, and they provided it. Tom could not drink because he was not allowed to drink. He was never alone. Very few families would be able to accomplish such a thing. He didn't like it, but he didn't have the strength to fight. They were exercising some tough love.

In some instances of drug and alcohol abuse interventions are necessary. An intervention is a form of "Tough Love." As many people as possible gather to tell the offender how his unacceptable behavior is disrupting or destroying the relationship he has with them personally. With bags packed and ready for the alcoholic, each participant in the intervention reads a prepared statement. The alternatives are to get help or get out.

Obviously interventions often produce hostilities and anxieties for everyone involved. They work best when people realize that giving people what they want is not always genuine love. Even if a person is arrested, loses his driving privileges or faces jail, he and everyone else is better off because then he cannot hurt himself or anyone else. Christ-motivated love is willing to take that step when it is absolutely necessary. In some cases this is enough to force a person to deal with the problem. Naturally, interventions are used by people who aren't Christians and don't know that Christ's love demands action like this in extreme circumstances. Still, Christ's love for everyone involved provides a motivation that cannot be duplicated, only imitated.

With the obvious benefits resulting from the use of gospel-motivated and law-directed love, one might wonder why we aren't inclined to use it more than we do. One reason might be that "Tough Love" could mean the end of a spiritual relationship with the church. But how much ministering are we doing if we fail to address real sins and provide the directions God's law gives? The risks may be great, but love that is unwilling to go the distance Christ went is actually self-serving, not Christlike. That kind of "Love" is more concerned about how we will feel if we act than it is about the actions God prescribes. The majority of people Christ addressed in the Gospels did not or would not hear him either. He wept over them because he was going to the cross to die for them. They didn't want what he was offering them, but he still showed them their sins so the opportunity was available to see their need for a cure.

Preparing the ground for the gospel is not easy work. It is hard enough to look at a church full of people and address specific sins in their lives. It is even more difficult to search until we find the sin in the life of the person in the counseling session, and then speak the law of God directly one to one. Sometimes that's the last counseling session you will be able to have with that person. You can lose a member of your congregation by speaking frankly about his sin. But so did many people turn away from Jesus because he wanted them to see that he was the Messiah, namely, the Savior from sin and the Lord of life. Many of them wanted only a superficial type of Messiah to solve superficial desires. Jesus even asked whether the disciples were among those who would leave him when the going got tough.

Peter's answer to the Lord is all the motivation we need to proceed directly and tactfully regardless of the consequences. Peter asked, "To whom shall we go? You have the words of eternal life." The law prepares the heart so we can plant the gospel. God will bless it in the way he sees fit to bless it. Unless we do our job with the law and then the gospel, God will have nothing to bless. Our skills are not the tools, God's word is. Each of the two major doctrines of Scripture, law and gospel, has a specific function according to the assignment God has given it. As God's undershepherds we need to pray that God would give us the courage, the insight, the wisdom and the words to communicate law so we are prepared to communicate the gospel in all our counseling.

CHAPTER FIVE
THE POWER OF THE GOSPEL TO PRODUCE RESOLUTION

When Naaman followed the advice of an Israelite girl to go to Elisha to be cured of his leprosy, he left Elisha disappointed. That was not Elisha's fault. Naaman was disappointed because Elisha didn't ask him to do something difficult, something expensive, something that would indicate how special Naaman's situation was. In effect, Elisha didn't ask him to do enough. If it had not been for the encouragement of the same girl, Naaman would have lived with his leprosy the rest of his life.

Elisha didn't even come out of the house. Naaman was supposed to wash in the Jordan river seven times. He had come ready to pay a king's ransom, but Elisha wanted nothing. In fact, Elisha didn't appear to do anything either. The whole situation made no sense to Naaman so he started home disappointed and angry. He decided he would get only what he paid for.

Naaman learned an important lesson. He learned that God didn't need his help to perform a miraculous cure. All Naaman needed to do was trust God to take care of his disease and let God do all the work. The power was all God's to cure Naaman. Elisha's presence, Naaman's money, even his willingness to go to the ends of the earth would accomplish nothing without God. Naaman thought he could help God, but he needed to learn he couldn't.

The story of Naaman is a good illustration of the power of the gospel to produce resolution. Gospel resolution is God's work. The account also provides a good illustration of why more people don't look to the gospel to provide the security and the peace God wants them to have. The gospel provides everything and demands nothing. That opposes human nature.

God left nothing undone when he planned and carried out his act of justification. From the first promise of a Savior, God was acting on behalf of people who could do nothing. When he kept eight people alive on the ark to preserve his promise, people did nothing to assist God in his work. When God promised Abraham a son, the patriarch and his wife Sarah could only believe God was telling them the truth. They couldn't help. God kept his promise in spite of the unfaithfulness of Israel. He not only proved the people could contribute nothing, he proved that his saving work would be completed even though his own people did everything they could to keep him from doing it. The Old Testament records God's work of free and faithful grace without the help of people and in spite of their failure to understand and appreciate what he was doing for them.

The four Gospels record the same truth. One reason Jesus' words and works did not appeal to the enemies of the Savior was because he did not allow them to contribute anything to his work on their behalf. He condemned their self-righteousness. He condemned the way Jewish leaders led God's people to trust their own legalistic works. They were blind people leading the blind.

The Apostle Paul brings the truth of God's free and faithful grace to its epitome in the letter to the Romans. In the first chapter he says the gospel is the power of God to everyone who believes. God's work saves, not man's. Jesus came, he lived perfectly, he died innocently and he rose victoriously. No one can add anything to what Jesus did. Everything else falls short of being acceptable to God. By comparison with what Jesus did, all the things people do or even try to do are dirty laundry and garbage where God's holiness is concerned. When we understand that, we understand the power of the gospel. God is doing the work, not we.

The gospel, in its simplest form, produced resolution for the keeper of the jail in Philippi who was about to die by his own hands. He was hopeless and helpless to do anything about his predicament. Even in that state of hopelessness he still tried to find a way to do something to save his life. "What must I do to be saved?" he asked.

In essence, Paul's answer was, "You can't do anything and don't have to, because God already did everything. Jesus completed his work. That fact exists for you to believe." God resolved the problem. The keeper of the jail did not die. Instead he and his family learned about life as they had never known it before, life with Christ.

The Bible is filled with examples of the way God teaches people to admit they can do nothing, but God has done everything. Nevertheless, that does not seem to stop people from trying to find some source of peace God might have overlooked.

Christians are just as likely as people who don't know the gospel to try to find ways to help God give them the peace they want. People who have never heard the gospel must turn to someone or something else other than God, because God to them is by nature an enemy, not a friend. Christians in their Old Adam have the same nature as non-Christians and to find peace are still as inclined as non-Christians to try alternatives to God's completed work.

No one has, as yet, produced a psychotherapy that builds on the reality that people are incapable of doing anything to obtain genuine peace. Most psychotherapies, in fact, define peace as generally normal human behavior and interaction with society. Peace with God is not in the picture at all. Because God is not in the picture, people can be content to find ways of obtaining peace that have nothing to do with God. They can simply decide what is normal and try to reach that goal.

For some people normality can be obtained by being oblivious to reality. If you have too many problems and too much stress to cope with, just take a pill or have a drink. From your point of view, at least, things will be bearable ("normal") for awhile. No wonder family, friends and counselors find it so difficult to get people to understand and accept their own substance abuse problems. Why should the alcoholic change? He has what he wants. His world looks just fine from his point of view. Thousands of alcoholics and substance abusers are willing to lose everything, including their lives, rather than give up their own illusion that everything is fine.

Substance abuse is not the only thing people use to justify their perspective of life. When people hurt enough they will want to change their behavior and find peace. The ways that appeal most to human nature are the ways that ask something of them or else tell them that the qualities for improvement lie within themselves. That is the way Naaman was thinking. Now we call it humanism. For that reason alone, the self-help books, tapes, programs, therapies and so forth are limitless. They all seem to have one thing in common. They all present some new idea for doing something or finding something within oneself that no one has thought of before. People never seem to tire of trying new ways to fail to find peace.

To one degree or another, this is humanism. Humanism teaches that people can pull themselves up by their own bootstraps. Think about that! If a person actually tries to pull himself up by his own bootstraps he will either break the straps or his back. He will not, under any circumstances, find true peace or even where "up" is for that matter.

The inclination to try to help God is part of human nature. Christians still have that sinful flesh, in spite of their new life in Christ. As a result, Christians at times have some unique ways of trying to do the same old things in a "Christian" way. How many times have you heard your people say they are looking for a Christian counselor? That's good, but what does it mean? Are they looking for a counselor who is a Christian himself? Are they looking for a person who will deal with them and their problem the way a Christian would? (How would a Christian deal with them?) Are they looking for someone who will tell them what God wants them to know, whether it sounds good or bad to them? If that's what they want, why should they not start with or at least include their own pastor? Why should their own pastor be content simply to refer them to someone else if the problem is spiritual in nature or at its roots?

The whole idea of trying to find peace apart from God is ludicrous. Simply using God's name on otherwise unscriptural material does not sanctify the material and give it the power the gospel has. Nevertheless, many pastors and teachers are content to turn to the yellow pages looking for someone who claims to be a Christian counselor without once bothering to find out whether the scriptural basis of law and gospel supports his work. Besides, the question of competence is not answered by the title "Christian." Many pastors are content to turn on a video or audiotape with a few disclaimers about heterodoxy, only to proceed to follow all the humanistic instructions this so-called "Christian" counselor gives.

Some so-called "Christian" counselors misquote Scripture to prove the humanistic points they want to make. In his book, *Peace of Mind through Possibility Thinking* (p. 150), for example, Robert Schuller supports his ideas about possibility thinking with the passage, "All things work together for good to those who love God *and keep his commandments*" (Romans 8:28. Schuller's addition italicized). What could be farther from the truth God intended for us in that passage? The passage has no power and offers no peace as Schuller uses it, to say nothing of the fact that God did not say it that way. The end result of listening to and believing the passage as it is quoted could never result in peace. It would lead to despair because a person would be confronted with the law he has not kept.

Persistent and unhappy people come to the office regularly with a new book, a new tape or information about a new workshop or seminar they have just learned about. Sometimes people have decided to be miserable. Sometimes they make up their mind what they want out of life, and they are waiting for God to deliver it on their terms. God has not always acted according to their whims. Occasionally they confront that fact. They know that what God wants for them is better than what they want, but still they continue to struggle with their unhappiness. They still don't feel good about themselves. As a result many have a library that fills bookcase after bookcase. They would be better off without a single book other than their Bible. Instead they insist on looking for something that tells them what they can be doing for themselves.

All the material people bring to me claims to be Christian, but the essence of much of it is work righteousness to one degree or another. As a result, these unhappy people not only struggle with their own feelings of inadequacy and self-esteem, they struggle with a constant battle between God's message to them and people telling them what they can try to do to help themselves. Those who use God's word to promote such self-help healing misuse the word and misguide troubled souls.

We have often heard that the world has only two different religions. On the one hand is Christianity, teaching that God does everything for our salvation. On the other hand is every other religion, teaching that people must do something themselves, ranging from a little bit to everything. One teaches the gospel, the other only the law. The Apostle Paul says the power to provide peace is in the gospel, and does not exist in the law. We understand that when we prepare sermons and lessons to teach God's people. It is just as true in counseling.

In our individual work we have the opportunity to determine whether we are communicating the power of the gospel. We have the opportunity to receive a response that helps us know whether or not the message has been received. We have the opportunity to apply the gospel to particular needs and situations in ways we cannot when talking to dozens or hundreds of people at once.

God made all the decisions when he created the world. The world didn't help. He spoke the word and creation happened. Lazarus made no decisions about whether or not he should come back to life. Jesus spoke the word and gave Lazarus the life he didn't have. No therapy, no book, no tape will do anything to add power to God's word. The gospel has the power to save, and with that salvation comes peace. That is precisely the reason we bring our people the gospel of peace in hospitals where they suffer from pain, illness and fear. The gospel provides peace no doctor can give. A doctor may be able to heal the body with God's help, whether or not he realizes God is doing the work. But a doctor does not have the tools in his medical knowledge to heal the soul. That is not his job, it's ours as God's workers.

The same thing holds true for emotional problems. Common sense and friendship, an ear ready to listen, and concern can do a lot to heal emotional wounds, but we must not forget about the soul. As in physical illnesses so also in emotional illnesses, personality disorders and mental illnesses, the soul is always involved. Every human being is both body and soul. Our concern is with the soul. In a literal, if not commonly used, sense we are psychologists (*i.e.,*"students of the soul"). We study the soul and the spirit of people. More than that, we have the tools to speak to the needs of the soul.

By contrast, many professional psychologists will not even acknowledge the existence of a soul. It is not their concern. But the soul is God's concern, along with the body. The gospel is the power that produces resolution because it applies God's answers, God's work and God's grace to body and soul. People cannot heal themselves, although they will try. Even Christians will try, though they know better. Our responsibility is to continue to present the gospel of free and faithful grace, the gospel that tells us God has done everything in Christ.

Peace is ours because God has done everything. The relief and resolution we and our people seek come from knowing that Jesus meant what he said on the cross: "It is finished." He was talking about his work for us and our people and the world. That's what we need to tell them again and again just as we need the reminder ourselves.

CHAPTER SIX
FINDING THE PROBLEM
THAT HINDERS RESOLUTION

How many psychologists does it take to change a light bulb? Only one, but the light bulb has to really want to change. That witticism identifies the problem of resistance, with which every counselor is familiar. Resistance, in counseling terms, means a person would prefer, for one reason or another, to leave an unacceptable or abnormal behavior the way it is. In other words, counselors cannot change a behavior, they can only guide people who want to make changes themselves.

One counseling service estimates that it helps 40% of the people who come for help. The service estimates that 60% of the people who present themselves for counseling don't want help in the first place. They come because other people think they should come. Many come because they think they are innocent victims of what others are doing to them. Some come thinking a counselor will be able to do something magical to help them improve the way they feel, without any effort of their own. After a few sessions the results are usually disappointing.

Psychology Today has stated that approximately 40% of the people in the United States need some kind of emotional help or support. Of that 40%, about 19% actually get the help they need. Of that 19%, approximately 20% actually improve. All of this illustrates that resistance plays an important part in counseling.

The problem of resistance is all the more severe where Christian counseling is concerned. Human nature has a strong and destructive resistance to both the law and the gospel. The natural resistance to the law and gospel is probably one of the primary reasons why people are willing to be satisfied with something less than genuine Christian counseling, if they really want help at all.

Resistance shows in different ways in counseling. For example, if a person is arrested for driving under the influence of alcohol, his sentence may include a period of time in rehabilitation and alcohol abuse education. That person may not be a particularly good candidate for rehabilitation. He is in rehabilitation because the court ordered it. He must fulfill the requirements of the court to reinstate his driver's license. Getting his license back may be his goal, not rehabilitation. Even his arrest and conviction may not convince him he has a drinking problem.

One form of resistance is denial. Denial is almost standard procedure among alcoholics. Lying goes hand in hand with denial. If one can lie to himself, why not lie to everyone else too? An alcoholic may hide liquor to cover up the evidence of drinking after promising not to drink. An alcoholic may refuse to admit a drinking problem even when drunk. One man I talked to refused to admit he had a drinking problem while he sat with me in his own home drinking from two beers open on the table in front of both of us. A lady refused to admit to drinking at all after her husband and I spent all night with her in a hospital in fear that she might stop breathing in her stupor. By the next morning she insisted on going home, still drunk. Within four hours she had filled with water the only bottle we could find in the house so it would appear she had not been drinking from it.

Jennifer exemplifies the resistance typical of alcoholics. She had serious problems. Everyone knew it but her. She presented forms of resistance on almost every level where counseling was attempted. She was both alcoholic and anorexic, a dangerous combination. She was thirty to forty pounds under her normal weight and still thought she was heavy. She knew she had a drinking problem, but considered it to be under control. Besides everything else, she was having marriage problems with a husband who was also an alcoholic. If anything, he encouraged her to continue drinking. Her two-year-old daughter was also showing signs of malnutrition that Jennifer refused to recognize.

Jennifer said she wanted to talk about her problems. I told her I would be happy to meet with her whenever she had a convenient time. The time never seemed to be convenient, but she wanted me to know that she still wanted to talk. Finally I decided that if we were going to meet, I would drive for an hour to meet her at the office where she worked. Her time was relatively free, but she was obligated to be at the office. I met with her three times for a total of nine hours under those circumstances. It could be considered a completely fruitless effort. It was probably not a wise way to begin counseling. I was motivated, but she wasn't.

The meetings at the office were not at all satisfactory. I asked what she thought was her biggest problem. She would state a problem. I would try to pursue it and she would change the subject. We continued to go around in circles this way until I could no longer tell whether she was resisting or whether she actually had a brain deficit resulting from her drinking and her improper diet.

If she had a brain deficit we would proceed more slowly and more patiently. If she was demonstrating resistance I would have to demand quick, stern confrontation. In consultation with a medical doctor, we decided against recommending a brain scan and some psychological testing. Instead we pursued a course that assumed that the problem was resistance. As a result, I refused to meet with her in any other setting than at my office on an appointment basis.

Jennifer did not make any serious attempts to make or keep any appointments even though her closest friends and relatives saw her problem getting worse by the day. We felt we could do nothing until Jennifer was ready to seek the help she needed. Only the Lord could have provided that willingness, and he did when Jennifer was hospitalized for a week with pancreatitis. A repeat of that episode in her condition would probably have cost her life. She was frightened enough to know she had to do something.

Psychiatrists, psychologists and substance abuse counselors in the hospital tried to encourage her to stay for inpatient substance abuse treatment. She said she wanted to handle her situation by counseling with me. Although it was a compliment, we had to consider the possibility that she chose this route because she thought I would be less competent to confront her problems than those in the clinical setting.

There was no question that those professionals were more qualified to deal with the problem. Her support group, however, agreed that the setting of the law and gospel was the only way to address the real problem. We all knew and accepted my limitations. I do not pretend to be a person who is trained in substance abuse counseling. We all agreed that with the support of a medical doctor and the guidance of a PhD who teaches substance abuse counseling, we would attempt to work with the problems. The first stage of resistance had been met and conquered. Jennifer was ready to come for help.

The first two or three sessions at my office were diagnostic. We tried to determine the underlying problem. In these first sessions all or part of Jennifer's support group was present. They brought her to the sessions and sat through them with her. Again we began to suspect that Jennifer was resisting counsel because her situation did not seem to be improving. Together we decided Jennifer would do better if she was responsible for coming to the sessions alone. At that point we reached level two of her resistance. She made an appointment and the day of the appointment called to say she could not keep the appointment because her husband had to take the car.

Under any other circumstances, unavailable transportation would seem like a reasonable excuse for missing an appointment, particularly with rather great distances involved. In this case, however, the counseling session and the appointment, promptness and dependability were key issues. Attendance at the counseling session meant Jennifer wanted help. Failure to attend meant she didn't want help. The first time the responsibility was left to Jennifer, she failed.

In consultation with her support group, we decided that strong and decisive action was necessary. I wrote a two-and-a-half page letter to Jennifer with copies to the members of her support group stating that I considered our counseling relationship terminated by her action. Her actions indicated that she did not want help or she would have been willing to come and get it. Instead, she had turned her desire for counseling and her relatives' concern into an opportunity to take advantage of them, while giving the impression that she was doing something about her problem. I told her I would be happy to work with her when she was ready to work. I hoped that would not mean ministering to her on her death bed. That was not an exaggeration. It was entirely possible. This was one of the most difficult steps I have ever taken. I wanted very much to help Jennifer, if only for the sake of the friends who cared so much about her; but the way things were going, we were not helping her, we were encouraging more self-destructive behavior.

None of us knew what to expect when the letter was sent. Jennifer called my office and home several times soon after she received it, but I did not take the calls. I wanted to see whether she would turn to her support group for help. To our surprise and thankfulness to God, Jennifer responded positively. She was very upset because she could not come for the help she wanted and needed. She realized her actions had been a ploy. She convinced the members of her support group that she really did want help and would work at it. They were convinced and we agreed to begin serious work on the problem. Jennifer never missed or was even late for another appointment after that. By the grace of God the second level of resistance had been met and conquered.

At that point level three of the resistance started. We openly confronted her drinking and her eating habits. She spent considerable time talking about the kind of circumstances that prompted her to want to drink. We identified the times when she did not feel like eating and when she purged food she had eaten. All of the occurrences had a common thread. They were stressful situations when she could not control what was happening at the moment. Those occurrences came so frequently, and Jennifer vomited so often, that she no longer had her own teeth at age 28. She had destroyed them with stomach acid.

Jennifer's self-abuse was a form of resistance too. She had learned to blame other people or things for making her drink and eat improperly. She would not believe she was responsible for her actions, but blamed other people instead. Getting past that point was at least as difficult as conquering the first two levels of resistance. Jennifer had to learn that situations and people cannot make someone act in a particular way. Jennifer's actions were her own choice and her own responsibility. Once again Jennifer needed to hear the law, but she was not used to hearing it spoken to her so directly.

By this time many counselors would feel they had finished their work. If Jennifer learned what was causing her problem, she would have reason and direction to change her behavior. In fact, she did change her behavior substantially. Drinking decreased radically, and eating increased proportionately. Some counselors would be satisfied with a change in behavior like that. We were all happy about it, but we knew we weren't finished. What other changes could counselors hope to obtain? They could hope for a change of heart and mind, a change of soul, repentance. Many counselors and psychologists, however, do not look for that kind of change.

Our work was not done. I met every hint of casting blame on someone else with opposition. Jennifer had to learn to accept responsibility for her actions even when a situation would make the most well-adjusted person angry. She would often respond, "Anybody would get angry about that. It's normal." She was right. Nevertheless, our response to that had to be, "Yes, but you are not every other human being. You did not come here to learn what everybody else would do in this situation. You came here to learn what God wants you to do and what he has equipped you to do." Finally Jennifer began to realize that her arguments produced no results and she began to acknowledge her own responsibility. Level three of her resistance had been met and conquered.

The one all-important step to healing still remained. Jennifer needed to learn what to do with the anger she felt. It didn't dissolve because she learned to control it. During our time together we had discovered and agreed that anger usually motivated her actions. She didn't know what to do with her anger except to take it out on herself. She punished herself for being angry by drinking and by not eating. She punished other people at the same time by making them watch her destroy herself. She wasn't getting what she wanted so she invented dangerous ways of getting attention from other people. That way she thought others would witness how much pain they were causing her. She was literally willing to kill herself to get that attention.

Jennifer knew that destroying her own body was a sin, but she didn't know what to do to resolve her anger. At that point we took another of those spiritual journeys to the cross. There at the cross she not only found forgiveness for her sins, but she also saw the Lord's forgiveness for the world. In other words, Jennifer didn't have the right to be angry with other people because the Lord had already forgiven them. She did not have the right to punish herself or other people because the Lord had already demanded punishment and exacted it from Christ. Instead of taking her anger out on other people and on herself, she learned to take it to the cross for the forgiveness Jesus had already won. She found the strength there to accept forgiveness for herself and the others around her who, she thought, were trying to hurt her. At that point Jennifer experienced a peace of mind and body she had never felt before. The entire reason for the way she was abusing herself was gone. Level four of her resistance had been met and conquered.

With the reason for her self-abuse gone, the only level of resistance remaining was to overcome the eating and drinking habits of almost twenty years. That in itself was no small problem. One-half to two-thirds of her life had been spent in self-abuse. Nevertheless, valuable professional assistance is available for facing that challenge. Only time will tell whether she will continue to use the strength God provides to handle her problem.

Jennifer's example illustrates well many of the kinds of resistance one will meet in Christian counseling. She thought counseling meant other people should do her work. She exhibited normal resistance common to substance abusers. She refused to face her responsibilities for her own actions. She resisted the law and the gospel. But by the grace of God all these resistances were met and conquered. The case is filled with evidence that counselors equipped with the power of God have a distinct advantage over those who aren't. God was guiding and directing the entire process that in many ways went well beyond the capabilities of the counselor and the support group.

On a much more familiar level, most counselors have had occasion to talk to one party alone while trying to deal with a marriage problem. None of us would question the desirability of having both parties present. When only one is present sessions can often turn into a detailed rehearsal of all the things that are wrong with the other person. Nothing could be more fruitless. Allowing this kind of discussion often violates the Eighth Commandment. It always stands in the way of finding the problem that hinders resolution.

For that reason alone, a counseling session cannot be an occasion for talking about what's wrong with someone who isn't there getting help. In my experience, the best way past such a problem is to insist that we talk about the problems the person present is having, as he or she deals with what the other is doing. In other words, "Let's talk about you and how you're doing. We can't do much to help someone who isn't here. Maybe you can learn how to help, even if your spouse won't come."

Perhaps the thought of helping the other party has not even occurred to the person in the office. He or she is usually more interested in the right to feel a particular way. To quote Jennifer again: "Isn't it natural to feel this way?" Yes, it may be natural, but these natural feelings may be prompted by hate and not by God-pleasing love. Those natural, sinful feelings must be dealt with if a person is to obtain resolution.

We can always expect to confront resistance in one form or another. It may not take all the forms of Jennifer's situation. It may take any one or several of them. Others may also appear. Forms of resistance should not surprise us when we meet them. If nothing else, we can expect to find resistance to the law and gospel, if only because it is the nature of every human being to resist God and his word.

We don't need to feel hopeless and helpless when we meet resistance. We shouldn't be surprised either. When God's word is the tool for the counseling we're doing, and God's will is the objective, we have a power and a guiding force that leaves everything less than genuine Christian counseling groveling in the dust.

Our tools are law and gospel from God's word. The cross is the key to the whole matter as it was for Jennifer. Our objective is to cut through the resistance in whatever form it appears so we can go to the cross to find the for-giveness we need for ourselves, or the forgiveness we need to give to others. Both kinds of forgiveness are available, but only at the cross of Christ.

CHAPTER SEVEN
FINDING A PRESENTATION
OF THE LAW
TO ADDRESS THE PROBLEM

Most people today will agree that guilt is a serious part of the problems people face. If this is the case, the biggest problem the secular counseling field has is what to do with guilt when it is evident. We face the same problem even though we are equipped with the gospel of full and free forgiveness. How do we find a specific way to address the sin troubling a person instead of simply making a generalized statement about sin and forgiveness?

Guilt comes in different forms, results from different sins and, consequently, needs different applications of the law and gospel. Simply reviewing the Ten Commandments may not be clear enough. Think, for example, of the people who came to Jesus thinking they had kept all the commandments, but still had doubts about their righteousness. Jesus often directed carefully worded parables to them to help them understand their sin. In our individual counseling we likewise have a special opportunity to take careful aim at a particular sin to address it with both law and gospel. That way we can confront the special needs a person has, even when he or she doesn't understand what that need is.

One time a girl, whose name I never knew and whom I never saw again, called to say she needed to talk to someone. When I met her at the church office, she was obviously very disturbed. She had a church home, another Lutheran church in the area. She came to me because she was ashamed and afraid to go to her own pastor, who knew her and her family on a personal basis.

The problem was easy to define. She had been pregnant. She understood her sin against the sixth commandment and had asked forgiveness for that. That sin did not trouble her. The problem was that she had had an abortion. For two or three weeks after the abortion she had been so troubled by what she had done that she returned to the clinic where the abortion was performed, because the clinic offered follow-up counseling. The people at the clinic told her that her depression was a normal part of this kind of surgery. They told her it was like the postpartum depression some women experience after childbirth. They told her she had made the right decision. Other friends she talked to seemed to support all this.

I asked her why, if she had already done so much talking with other people, did she want to talk to me. She said she still felt guilty. I asked her what she felt guilty about. She said she felt she had committed a murder. Had she talked about that with anyone else? She hadn't. She couldn't because no one wanted to talk about abortion that way.

I told her she had committed murder. The life she asked her doctor to take was a human life. She was actually glad to hear that because she could deal with that sin against the fifth commandment the same way she had dealt with her sin against the sixth commandment. She could seek

God's forgiveness. When I assured her of that forgiveness she went away with a peace she had not experienced for weeks. She was like the woman taken in adultery who was brought to Jesus to be judged guilty, but heard him say, "Then neither do I condemn you. . . . Go now and leave your life of sin" (John 8:11). My personal belief, although I have no way of knowing, is that she never had another abortion and never had a reason to need one.

This example only serves to illustrate the ways people themselves and, in particular, counselors deal with guilt when they are not equipped with the gospel. The best one can do is to try to take the sinfulness out of the sin. People will excuse it, rationalize it, hide it, and, in short, use any means available to remove guilt by denying sin.

On the other hand, people often carry guilt for things the law does not say are sinful. Many pastors have had the experience of seeing whole families or family members sit for hours or days while a loved one was unconscious and terminally ill in the hospital. The strength they need, either to cope with the difficulties of recovery, or to endure everything involved with a death, is sapped by sleeping in chairs in a hospital room. If they can sleep at all, they just wait for something to change. Encouraging them to go home and take care of themselves only produces a response like, "I would feel so guilty if I were not here with him when he died." Nevertheless, even at times like that, the family frequently is not present when death comes.

A man had brain surgery and appeared at first to be doing well. His condition reversed and he began to decline rapidly. The family was with him at the hospital night and day for several days constantly hoping, losing hope and then hoping again. The family members didn't feel they could leave with the situation in such a state of flux. Finally the doctor insisted that all the equipment keeping the man alive should be turned off. The man's brain was dead.

Was the family doing the right thing by signing the papers? The doctor was very helpful in explaining that the man's brain had ceased to function. The only signs of life were being produced by the life support equipment. After a great deal of thought and prayer for God's guidance, the family agreed. Even with that, some members of the family insisted on being with their father after the life support was eliminated. It was a long and agonizing twenty minutes watching several monitors, seeing vital signs deteriorate and ultimately hearing the doctor pronounce the man dead. The time could easily have been much longer.

A year later we went through the whole situation step by step again with the man's wife. She still wondered whether she was guilty of murder. She had not really confronted her guilt. She had been too exhausted. She heard so many rational explanations that she never thought about the guilt she was feeling. She didn't want to think about whether or not she was doing the right thing. No one else wanted her to have to deal with those thoughts either. Besides her problems, the others had emotions of their own to deal with.

I can remember going through some guilt of my own in the same situation. I was called to be with the family most of Saturday night and went home just in time to conduct Sunday services. I was called back to the hospital shortly after church was over. I returned to the hospital when the decision was being made to terminate the extreme medical measures. I stayed with family members in the intensive care unit to watch as the vital signs dropped and finally ceased. That day was also the day my oldest daughter was confirmed. Either being at home or being at the hospital would have been the wrong place as far as others involved were concerned. Fortunately my daughter under-stood the problem, and, if I made a decision contradicting God's will, I believe God has forgiven me too.

The point of these examples is that guilt is not always definable according to the law of God, and yet, the guilt is real. We may not be able to say an action is a sin against any commandment in particular and yet people still feel guilty. The temptation arises to try to dismiss the guilt as unfounded and unreal. Perhaps it is Satan's way of con-demning people without a cause. In some cases simple reassurance of God's faithfulness in the face of Satan's lies is enough to produce resolution of the problem. But in the cases mentioned above, simply saying the doctors had done everything they could do and life was in God's hands was not enough. Saying you can't be in two places at once and you must set priorities was not enough. Other matters had to be addressed with the law and the gospel. No amount of rationalizing could get rid of it.

In both the case of the people who had to sign papers to cease life support and the personal situation of trying to be in two places at the same time, the sin against the first commandment showed itself clearly. Only God decides the limits of life. He alone can give it and take it. The doc-tor indicated that God had taken this life, and no amount of hoping or medical equipment could reverse God's decision. In the other example, only God is omnipresent and my presence at either location was not as important as God's presence at both. The sins are obvious and the facts are humbling, but the facts do address the real underlying problem. Those sins must be addressed to find resolution.

While some guilt may be as obvious as the murder of an unborn child, we can easily fall into the trap of helping our people do the very thing we would discourage them from doing under other circumstances. When we fail to understand the real underlying sin, when we fail to seek it, discover it and reflect it against the mirror of the law, we may be just as inclined as a non-Christian counselor to try to rationalize the sin. That helps no one. Helping those who suffer from depression offers a good example of this problem which all Christian counselors face.

The market teems with books on coping with depression. Most of them, Christian as well as secular, have one overriding warning, *don't talk about guilt*. The person feels bad enough already. The person probably feels guilty already. Don't talk more about guilt and make matters worse. If a person already feels guilty, as some of these books suggest, then why avoid talking about the guilt? Guilt may be the source of the depression in the first place.

Most material on the subject of depression points to some kind of loss as one of the culprits. This could be the loss of a loved one, a job, self-esteem, a future hope, or other losses of this kind. Because of their particular loss, people feel depressed, literally pressed down.

Indications of depression are often physical as well as emotional. A person may not feel like going to bed at night or may not be able to wait until it is time to go to bed. He or she may not want to get up in the morning. Work is either boring or too demanding. One way or another he or she doesn't seem to be able to get much of anything done. When the situation gets so bad that normal activities such as eating, going to work, getting out of bed and taking care of oneself virtually cease, a person may be considered clinically depressed. He or she may need medical attention. Under some circumstances people have already sought medical attention because of nagging illnesses, aches and pains, and general discomfort. Such symptoms may also be an indication of depression. If a person chooses to talk to the Christian counselor about the problem, guilt seems to be the last thing he would want to talk about.

Perhaps the general root problem could be redefined for our purposes. Instead of speaking of a loss, the depressed person might say, "I'm not getting what I want," or, "I don't have what I want anymore." Looking at it from that point of view, depression can be and often is a selfish and self-centered form of emotional distress. "I" frequently seems to be at the center of the problem. When the "I's" begin to come out in the conversation, we will have difficulty avoiding the need to address guilt. Once again, the first commandment says, in paraphrase, that what "I" want is not as important as what God wants.

Depression often produces copious tears. In fact it is probably the main reason I always make sure I have a box of tissues on my desk. Some people have even offered to replace them because they used so many. Nevertheless, when the tears come, we're probably starting to get close to the root problem. Consciously or unconsciously, the person already knows what it is. He or she may not want to admit it, or may not understand it, at first; but the tears are more than just a vent for the emotions. They may begin a flood of words defining the real problem.

After a seminar on depression I conducted in our congregation, a lady slipped a note to me saying she wanted to talk about her depression. I might add that of some twenty-five seminar topics offered for discussion, depression was far and away the number one subject chosen.

Ruth, the lady who slipped me the note, made an appointment and began with a description of how miserable she was in her marriage. She enjoyed travel and had traveled a great deal before her marriage at about age thirty. She enjoyed traveling with her husband; but now she had three children, so Ruth and her husband were not as free as they had been before. Besides the lack of freedom, Ruth's husband was not as helpful as he had been before. He spent most of his time at work. He didn't help with the children, although he was very good with them, perhaps better than Ruth herself. He didn't get projects done around the house. A planned addition to the house was five years in building and still incomplete although the family had no lack of funds. Most of the discussion centered around Ruth's husband failing to live up to Ruth's expectations.

As the first session drew to its close, Ruth and I agreed that little could be done to change her husband, particularly because he was unwilling to meet with us. He didn't think a problem existed. If it did, it was Ruth's problem, not his. That meant Ruth and I would have to work alone toward a solution. She couldn't change the situation.

As we began to understand Ruth's problem and her background, she seemed to be indicating, whether she knew it or not, that her husband was not the problem, but the children. She didn't have the freedom she wanted because they restricted her. We talked about what her own childhood was like, particularly because she said her sister was also seeking counsel for depression. Ruth was the second of three children. Her sister was the youngest and her brother was the oldest. Ruth had an especially unhappy childhood. She wasn't close to her mother because her mother drank to excess and was all but oblivious to the children, if not resentful of them.

Ruth's father was the dominant figure. From Ruth's perspective and her sister's, her brother could do nothing wrong, and they could do nothing right in their father's eyes. Ruth resented him for this. She felt her father wished the two girls didn't exist.

I asked Ruth how she handled her feelings about her father. She said she did everything she could to block them out of her memory, but when she talked about her childhood, the tears began to flow freely.

I asked her if she could see any similarity between her childhood and the relationship she had with her own children. Then the flood gates opened. She was recreating her own childhood in her own family because she had come to resent her children in the same way she had experienced her father's resentment. Ruth's depression did not come from her difficulties with her husband, they were coming from her attitude toward her own children, which was just like her father's attitude toward her. Ruth was not mourning the loss of her freedom, she was mourning the loss of the affection of her father. She felt like she never had a father. When she came to that realization, she said through the tears, "That's just what I didn't want to happen."

When Ruth realized what was really at the root of her problem, the next steps involved looking at her children as blessings, not as restrictions. She could now take a personal trip to the cross. She could forgive her father for his failings and find forgiveness for her own resentment. She looked to her husband for support and he usually provided it. The tension between husband and wife diminished and the two appreciated each other's company more. Her husband found that being at home could be enjoyable.

The children became more involved in what Ruth and her husband did. They no longer needed to be away from the children as much as they had been before. Ruth started finding more enjoyment in doing things with the children instead of constantly running after them to pick up the messes they had made. Ruth had been angry with her father for years and had refused to forgive him. When that problem was resolved almost everything else improved.

On another occasion, a man called the office about his wife who seemed emotionally distraught. She cried constantly, sometimes for no apparent reason. Her husband was sure she needed help, but wasn't sure where to get it. We agreed to try to talk to his wife, and, to his surprise, she was quite willing to talk.

At first Sarah came alone. She was middle-aged and exhibited quite a bit of the emotional instability Steven had described. She cried almost the entire first session. We agreed that one of the simplest actions she could take would be to have a thorough medical examination, which she had not had for some time. Perhaps her age and the change of life had something to do with her problem. The examination by the doctor indicated that Sarah's problems were not medical. Her doctor did not suggest supplemental hormones or other medication for her condition.

In many of the things that upset Sarah, her husband, Steven, seemed to be a factor. Both of them had gone through the problem long enough to want to do anything they could to alleviate it. Most of the early sessions, however, offered little progress. We decided that perhaps some psychological testing would be valuable. The *Wechsler Personality Inventory* was a simple test the couple could fill out in the office. In turn, through previous arrangements, we sent it to a psychologist. His office staff provided a computerized analysis.

While awaiting the results of the testing, as sort of a last resort, I asked each of the two to tell me, if they could, what their earliest recollections were. Sarah immediately burst into tears. "I haven't thought of this for years." The first thing she could remember was when her mother died and she was watching the casket being taken from their home to the cemetery. Steven, on the other hand, remembered playing in the woods and being stuck in some sticky mud or quicksand.

These two early recollections had remarkable significance. The essence of Sarah's early recollection was of someone leaving. Since then people had been leaving her time and again. One of her daughters left to be married. Shortly after that her older daughter died. Other events in her life were just as significant. Someone was always leaving her. As a result she held onto people fiercely and didn't want anyone to leave her again.

Her husband, on the other hand, was the exact opposite. He couldn't stand to be "stuck" by someone holding onto him. The more his wife depended on him, the more he felt stuck the way he had felt as a youngster in the quicksand. Steven's recent heart attack had increased Sarah's feelings of insecurity and simultaneously increased his desire for independence. Without realizing it, the two were working against each other. When the psychological evaluations came by return mail, they confirmed what we had already learned.

The problems in the marriage were becoming clearer. The guilt both parties were experiencing came from misunderstanding the needs of the other. They began to see more clearly how important they were to each other, not from the standpoint of depending and being depended on, but from the standpoint of giving themselves to each other to supplement what the other lacked. Sarah had more than enough compassion and empathy to share with Steven, and Steven knew how to be independent much better than Sarah did. They realized God couldn't have done a better job of making two people right for each other so they could give to each other instead of taking. The insecurities that lay hidden for so many years were resolved, and the peace the couple experienced became an opportunity for sharing.

Anxiety is a close cousin to depression. In some cases the physical and emotional symptoms can be almost the same. One can easily be mistaken for the other. While depression seems to deal more with a loss of some kind, or to put it another way, "I'm not getting what I want,"

71

anxiety comes more from things beyond our control. Efforts to control the uncontrollable cause people anxiety.

For a number of reasons the anxiety factor may be more evident in our present society than at other times in history. People seem to feel more of a need and more of a right and expectation to be able to control their own lives, the lives of others and even life itself. For example, people face terminal illness and the difficulties it causes in different ways than in years gone by. People can easily expect medical science to be able to cure anything with a pill or an operation. We can control pain and tension, stress and stress-related illnesses with medications to control anxiety. More than half of the psychiatric medication available is specifically designed to reduce stress or anxiety in one way or another.[1] In a sense, we are in a society that doesn't believe people should have to suffer emotionally or physically, and, to a degree, does not even accept that people die, and that no one can change the inevitability of it.

Facing a terminal illness as a patient involves a grieving process not unlike the process following the death of a loved one. On the part of those facing the illness with a loved one, the grieving process may actually take place twice, once before and once again after death.

One young lady, Betty, was a cancer patient. Her condition was terminal. She, as is often the case, did a better job of coping with her illness than those around her. Her closest relationship was with her husband and her infant son. Besides that she had sisters and brothers, sisters-in-law and brothers-in-law. In addition, she lived near her childhood home and family, so her parents and even some aunts and uncles were close by. All of these people had things to say about Betty's illness and the way she was

---

[1]Cf. *Physicians' Desk Reference,* Product Category Index, Medical Economics Co., Ordell, NJ, 1990, pp. 201-227.

handling it. All of them had something to say about the way others were dealing with it. Often the situation was tense and even hostile.

Very few, if any, of the people involved understood what the real problem in the relationship was. They were too close to see the obvious. All of them were angry with God for letting this happen to someone who was so important to all of them. None of them wanted to admit their anger with God and with the illness. None of them wanted to face the real sin of trying to take control away from God and into their own hands. All of them tried to do something other than admit that their situation was beyond their control and in the hands of God. They couldn't say all things were being done well because they weren't letting God do anything. He is the only one who can do all things well.

Another lady, Leona, also suffered from cancer and faced death because of it. Her husband stayed with her day and night for weeks. Eventually he became irritated with her because he and others thought she should be doing more than she was to try to fight her illness. For more than a month she refused to talk to anyone. This only created more frustration for her husband.

One day while her husband was briefly out of the room and she was still refusing to respond to anything, even so much as to say the Lord's Prayer during a devotion, I told her I didn't know what was going on in her mind, but I didn't have the feeling that she was experiencing sorrow over her situation. I thought she was angry. I thought she was angry with her husband, with her doctor, with herself, with her illness, with me as a representative of God and finally with God himself. This produced a flood of words and tears that had been welling up inside her for weeks. She had been angry with God. She didn't understand how he could let this happen to her. Most of all, she didn't want to admit to being angry with the God she loved and trusted. When she did release the guilty feelings at the cross, she could experience the forgiving love of the God she had been growing to hate. The tension was gone.

Another man was stricken with cancer. Vince's cancer progressed so rapidly that he died in less than three months. He and his family were fighting with the determination to hold on in a situation that was growing more hopeless by the day. Vince had not been a member of any church, although he had a Catholic background. He was a neighbor and a friend, but never had anything to do with the church.

One day Vince's daughter called and said he wanted to talk with me alone when he got home from the hospital. Soon she called again and said he may not come home from the hospital, and I shouldn't wait to talk with him. In the course of fifteen minutes with Vince we answered one simple question on his mind. He asked, "What do I have to do?" His question sounded very much like the question addressed to the Apostle Paul by the jailer at Philippi. I had the privilege of telling him he didn't have to do anything because everything was already done by Jesus. During that fifteen minutes an almost unbelievable calm came over him and, consequently, over his family. He died at peace, because he had faced his hidden sins and God had dealt with them for him. He died a Christian who knew and trusted his Savior to control what he couldn't control.

Besides illnesses, daily stress and anxiety take serious physical tolls. One doctor, a pulmonary specialist (heart and lungs), suggests that 50% to 75% of his patients suffer from diseases related to anxiety. Gastroenterologists (the digestive system) often quote similar percentages. A number of books on the market also indicate how concerned people are about controlling their lives, or at least learning how to control their ways of dealing with life. As a nation we seem to be facing a growing deception that we have more control over our lives than we do.

All the physical and emotional disorders this anxiety causes cannot be adequately addressed here. We will attempt to deal with some of them later. We can say this much, however: we cannot expect the secular market to do our job of telling people it is a sin to try to control what is in God's hands and is his alone to control. God does not suffer from anxiety. Neither is he a God of anxiety. That would be impossible because nothing is beyond his control. If confronting the sin helps us to get that message across we will be able to help people find resolution to their problems much better than anything or anyone else can.

Confronting sin may be a difficult task, particularly when we deal with people who are suffering from severe emotional strain. Their tears, their sorrows, their anxieties, their illnesses can all make a counselor shy away from addressing guilt. But our intention is not to make matters worse. Our prayer is that we can resolve the problem with God's help and God's word. We cannot do that without learning what sin hinders resolution. We don't have to be afraid to look for underlying guilt because, unlike the secular community, we know the gospel resolves guilt. We can give them God's peace.

THE TRIP TO THE CROSS
THAT PRODUCES RESOLUTION

Justification by grace through faith in Jesus Christ is the central doctrine of Christianity. Justification is God's declaration that the world is counted righteous in his sight only because of Jesus' redemptive work. God declared the innocent Christ guilty so he could pronounce the guilty world innocent. Because God has pronounced this verdict we have the privilege to tell anyone and everyone their sins have been fully and freely forgiven for the sake of the Lord Jesus Christ. Christians who are faithful to the word of God make such a pronouncement in one form or another in every sermon they preach or every visit they make.

This chapter is intended to emphasize justification more fully and completely in the counseling work we do. To accomplish this, I would like to focus on the healing value of Christ's redemption that makes justification by grace through faith a reality.

Christ's work of redemption makes God's declaration of justification well-grounded. By redeeming the world from sin, death and the power of the devil, the God-Man satisfied both God's justice and his mercy at the same time. God's justice was satisfied because Christ carried the sins of the world and paid for them in full. God's mercy was satisfied because the payment was made by his own Son, the God-Man Jesus Christ, and not by any other human being.

Christ's work of redemption is a finished product, and that makes God's declaration of justification by grace through faith the final word on the subject. For that reason, the Apostle John says in 1 John 3:19-20, "This then is how we know we belong to the truth, and how we set our hearts at rest in his presence whenever our hearts condemn us. For God is greater than our hearts, and he knows everything." The apostle brings out some points that deserve emphasis. First, he is talking about people who belong to the truth. He is talking about believers. Second, John states that even Christians' hearts sometimes condemn them. People need to know and be reminded continually, even as Christians, that they have full and free forgiveness in Jesus Christ. Christians need that because they too are subject to the lies of Satan and are responsible for their own actions. Both Satan's lies and our own thoughts, words and actions produce guilt. Third, John points out that the heart is not the final authority on the matter of guilt or innocence. God is. And last, the apostle directs us to God, who declares us righteous, as the one who "knows everything." That declaration stands in the face of the lies of Satan, the pangs of a conscience that can err, or even the evidence of sin judged by God's law itself. That declaration has the power and authority to put the heart at rest.

Forgiveness is easy to declare. All faithful preachers talk about forgiveness. The problem is that we usually talk about it only as a final declaration without emphasizing the process Christ completed to make the declaration valid. If a person confesses a particular sin to a pastor or counselor or friend, for example, the counselor can easily declare forgiveness and assure the sinner that the sin is forgiven. That is the truth. It is God's truth and it will not change. What we may forget, however, is that the person may have been going through an entire mental process of payment for sin. The counselor has perhaps delivered the answer to the problem without making a vivid presentation of the process Jesus completed for obtaining the solution.

Even the best of the Christian writers often ignore this obvious point. Lawrence J. Crabb, one of the finest writers in the field of Christian counseling and psychology, for example, speaks highly of the importance of atonement, God's unconditional love. He talks about the finished work of Christ and the truth and certainty of it, often without the vivid details the Bible provides for how Christ made all this a reality. That is the point that deserves our attention. That is the trip to the cross that produces resolution.

The Bible clearly teaches an opinion of the natural law within every human being that demands some kind of payment for a wrong. We are familiar with the self-righteousness of the Pharisees who attempted to make it virtually impossible to break the law. Their Sabbath laws, their laws restricting work and diet, their constant attempts to justify any and every act show clearly that they knew sin demanded payment. Their acts of open and public righteousness show the ways they chose to deal with the problem. Even at that, some of the Pharisees came to Jesus with legitimate questions about what more they needed to do to find peace they didn't have. All their efforts did not satisfy the demands of the natural or the written law.

Before his conversion, the Apostle Paul was tortured by a zeal to do more than anyone would demand or expect. After his conversion he was fully aware of the uselessness of his struggle. Before the Reformation, Luther struggled mightily with what happens to people who believe that righteousness is obtained by works.

We could go on indefinitely with proofs that the law demands a payment for sin. The point is that the gospel speaks constantly of the payment Christ made, and so should we who faithfully proclaim it. Yet, all too often we do not review how the payment was made, as God presents it to us. We are content to provide only the final solution, "Your sins are forgiven." The Bible does much more than that. It shows us the process Christ went through to do the work we will naturally try to do by ourselves. Scripture parallels Christ's work and ours to show us that Christ's work actually made the payment where ours couldn't. We need to do the same thing in our presentation of the gospel. We need to take the time to present the process, redemption, payment; and then we need to make the final declaration on God's behalf as he gave us the authority to give it. "*And so*, your sins are forgiven."

By this time all this is sure to seem pitifully obvious. Nevertheless, I believe strongly that we fail to recognize numerous occasions when our people are in the process of making their own payment for sin in their own chosen way and are closed to the presentation of the gospel, because they don't see it as the answer to their needs. The final declaration means virtually nothing to those who are in the process of making spiritual payment on their own, some other way.

Some illustrations of the ways people have used to make payments for their sins may help clarify the point. When reading the penitential psalms, particularly Psalm

32 and Psalm 51, the reader cannot help noticing the emotional as well as the spiritual distress David endured while carrying the guilt of his adultery with Bathsheba and consequent murder of Uriah. The king of Israel would have been pronounced clinically depressed if he were living in our day. He would probably be treated with antidepressants. He would be placed into intensive therapy. He would be force-fed in a hospital setting because he was a man who was literally being crushed by his own guilt. He wouldn't eat, he couldn't sleep. He was virtually non-functioning.

If Elijah lived in our day, he too would be marked as clinically depressed, a candidate for hospitalization because of his suicidal insinuations. After his confrontation with the prophets of Baal he felt hopelessly alone, completely incapable of more work for the Lord, and, besides that, his life was in jeopardy.

Jonah, as we see him ask God to take away his (Jonah's) life in the fourth chapter of his prophecy, might also be considered suicidal and desperately in need of emotional and spiritual care. He disagreed with the Lord's assignment for him and the way the Lord blessed his work.

In all these cases God took care of both the spiritual and the emotional needs of his people. He did it with a process, not a simple declaration. God provided the assurance of forgiveness, and also showed them why he could put away their sins.

The signs of a person in the process of following the natural law within him are many and varied. They may be mild or dangerously severe. They may appear as medical problems. They may appear as depression. They may appear as some kind of -holism, alcoholism, workaholism, obsession, compulsion and the like. For this reason many people confuse the symptom with the problem. For example, if you can cure the alcoholism the other emotional problems will go away. Most likely the opposite is true. If the person eats better he will consequently feel better. But what if the person is not eating because he is trying to starve himself to death slowly, to make his own personal atonement for a sin he cannot identify or does not know *how* to deal with in any other way? Judas tried to pay for what he had done to Christ by taking his own life. From his perspective, a life for a life was the only possible payment. As a result he faithlessly lost the benefit of the work Christ completed the very next day, when he made the ultimate and perfect payment.

One person, Charles, was a very conscientious individual. He wanted to do the best he could with his job. But his work presented many daily demands for almost superhuman strength and wisdom. He usually felt he was failing at his work. More and more was left undone. That only made matters worse.

Since Charles was in the full-time work of the church, he had a thorough knowledge of Scripture and the truths it presents. In spite of that knowledge Charles continued to decline in his effectiveness and in his physical health. Soon his health, severe digestive problems, forced a leave of absence. That leave seemed to be the exact opposite of what needed to be done. To Charles the solution was to work harder. Yet his body couldn't tolerate the demands. Eighteen hours a day seemed to be too much to expect, but reducing the work load and restricting his time only served to compound the problem. The less he was allowed to work, the more people expressed their concerns about his work load, the worse his health became.

The fact was that Charles was punishing himself for not being able to do what he expected of himself. Less work meant more emotional and physical punishment. More work meant more emotional and physical punishment. Doctors told Charles that without a serious change, death was imminent. In other words, Charles was slowly committing suicide. He was not holding a gun to his own head. He was not threatening to slash his wrists. He was overdosing on his work.

The solution to the problem came only when Charles understood the process of redemption designed by God specifically for him. In this case that process was revealed through the well-known passage in 2 Corinthians where Paul spoke in chapter twelve about his own thorn in the flesh. Many people have spent reams of paper discussing why the apostle would talk about his vision of heaven in the third person and about his thorn in the flesh in the first person. The answer seems obvious. The text makes it clear Paul was talking about himself in the third person. But as a human being Paul couldn't afford to be exalted above measure because of the revelation of heaven he received in his ministry for Christ. The Lord consequently allowed him to suffer some kind of thorn in the flesh. Conveniently, the apostle does not identify what that thorn in the flesh was. That allows us to plug in almost any thorn we might experience personally, without doing violence to the text.

God had a reason for giving Paul both the thorn in the flesh and the revelation. Paul the apostle needed a revelation of heaven to see the importance of the work God had given him to do even in the face of persecutions. He was compelled to do the work of preaching the gospel because he had experienced the glory he was sharing with those in his care. Paul the human being, on the other hand, needed something else from God. Paul the human being needed total dependence on God to provide the strength for the work he was doing. God provided the goal, but God also provided the means to the goal. All of us know the need for that humble dependence, but even the Apostle Paul failed to apply it to himself without a specific lesson.

This understanding made all the difference in the world to Charles in his condition. He was doing what so many pastors, teachers and counselors try to do. He was not only serving God, he was trying to serve as God.

God has a multitude of ways to let us know he is God and we are not. The situation Charles faced with continuing digestive problems offered much more opportunity for reflection on the problem than a severe heart attack, which could just as well have been the result of his thought and work patterns. God exercised enduring patience with Charles. Charles knew upon graduation from the seminary that he was in God's work, but he had not yet learned that he was not capable of doing the work instead of God. Furthermore, he wanted to be faithful so he tried for all he was worth to do the work only God could do. Charles was flesh and blood, a limited human being like Paul, who needed total dependence on God more than relief for illness. He found it in the forgiveness of God for the sin of acting not as God's spokesman, but as God.

The lesson was long and difficult and dangerous, but God was very patient. The results could have easily been an instant massive heart attack, an instant cerebral hemorrhage due to high blood pressure, or serious respiratory problems. All these things have their roots, in some cases, in stress, trying to control what we cannot control. What more likely place for them to show than when we are guilty of trying to do God's work for him, since he has already told us to give it to him. Predictably, Charles' health problems disappeared when he realized the difference between being faithful to God and being faithful as a human god.

What is true of pastors, teachers and other counselors is also true of people in their congregations. We cannot ignore that God deals with us in his word and in our lives with a process. As it was not enough to tell Charles he was forgiven, as it was not enough to deal only with the digestive problems, as it was not enough to deal only with the work load, so it is not enough to spend forty-five minutes with a person and tell him his sins are forgiven and expect everything else to get better. The result of that action is the common misconception that all this is simply a weakness of faith. Now we have one more thing to feel guilty about. We have a weak faith on top of everything else. Of course we have a weak faith. God knows that and he works constantly to strengthen it. It is God's strengthening we need to concentrate on, not our weakness.

The doctrine of redemption parallels our own efforts to pay for our sins, known or unknown, with the way Christ dealt with them for us. Redemption works, but our efforts don't. Once the law shows us the root problem, the gospel of redemption shows us what Christ did about it. It also shows us that Christ succeeded where we necessarily fail. That is the message we really want to communicate in our counseling offices and our pulpits. We already know people will try to find a way to pay for their sins. They may pretend they don't care about them, but there is too much stress in our society and among our people to ignore the obvious. By nature they will strive mightily to make everything right on their own. We need to work just as hard and harder, in countering human nature, to find a way to show them that Christ already paid for sins, while human beings can't.

Any of the examples cited previously would serve as illustrations for the process we are considering. A specific selection of an exemplary problem is unnecessary because the process works the same way whenever a sin is uncovered and needs resolution. In chapter three, for example, we met Connie, the lady who suffered from a form of paranoia. We saw how she tried to deal with her guilt by using her paranoia. We saw her attempts to find ways to get God to give her the strength to carry her own problems. In her case, telling her God had forgiven her sins, whatever they were, was not enough. She was too deeply involved with the process of trying to pay for the sins herself.

As we sat in the office exchanging ideas about how to get rid of the guilt and how much more she could do to try to handle the situation, we talked about Matthew 11 and the rest Jesus speaks about in verse 29. But that was just the beginning. Obvious questions still remained.

What kind of rest was Christ talking about? He was talking about rest from all this guilt she was carrying, and all the ways she was trying to find to do a better job of carrying it. What should she do about all those weights? She should lay them down. Where would she take them? She would take them to Jesus. Where could she find Jesus telling her in the clearest possible way that he really wanted her to lay them down? She would have to go to the cross of Christ. What would she find at the cross? She would find her suffering Savior. Why was he suffering? He was suffering for her. What was he suffering? He was suffering pain, the agony of hell and death for her. How did the suffering she was experiencing compare with what Jesus did? Her suffering didn't begin to compare with what Jesus had done. How did she know Jesus had done all this for her? She could go to the cross and see her sins there. How did she know Jesus had finished paying for her sins? He said he was finished paying for them. How did God prove Jesus was finished paying for her sins? Jesus rose from the dead. Did Jesus make enough of a payment for her sins to allow her to lay them all at the cross? He certainly did. He paid for all sins. How would she describe Jesus' work of paying for her sins? He was completely successful.

How was she trying to pay for her sins? She was suffering from paranoia and constant guilt feelings. What good was this accomplishing? She only got worse. What had she done to try to get better? She had tried numerous ways to get rid of her feelings, including seeing a psychiatrist, using prescribed medication, not sleeping at night, not being able to work during the day, feeling guilty because she couldn't do her work, ruining her marriage and family life, making people miserable, driving people away from her, and in general, being a real nuisance to everyone. How was this process working for her? It wasn't working at all. How were things improving? Things weren't improving, they were deteriorating rapidly.

How would she compare the way Christ handled her problems and the way she handled them? His way worked and her way didn't. Which of the two would give her what she wanted? Only Jesus could give her what she wanted. How would she get what Jesus had won for her? She would believe he had done it for her.

With the increasing knowledge and faith that Jesus had already taken care of her problems on the cross, Connie realized the rest that Jesus promised her. Her guilt was removed. She was at peace with God and with herself. The paranoia was gone, she felt a thousand pounds lighter. She was anxious to get home and tell her family what had happened. She would apologize to her husband and family and believe they accepted her apologies. She would do her housework. She would sleep at night. She would reduce her medication under the direction of the doctor. Jesus did what no one else could have done, but she had to know how he did it before she could accept the fact that he did it.

The same situation existed in the case of Ruth, the lady who was depressed and didn't know why. She learned she was really depressed because of her feelings about her father. She had hated him from little on, but she didn't know what to do with her resentment. She not only needed forgiveness, she needed the strength to forgive someone who was no longer alive. She could not deal with the situation by talking with him. She had to resolve the matter in her own mind and with God both emotionally and spiritually.

How did she feel about her father? She was still angry with him. What would she do with that anger? She would have to get over it. How would she get over it? She would work harder. What would she do? She would try harder not to be like him. How would that help her feelings about her father? Maybe she could learn to appreciate him by learning what not to do in her family. How was that process working? It wasn't working at all. What showed her plan was not working? The more she tried to be different, the more angry she became that he had put her through all this.

In what way could God help in the situation? God could help her learn to forgive. What could God help her learn to forgive? He could help her learn to forgive her father for what he had done. What else could he do? He could guide her to being the good mother she wanted to be. What was she doing to obtain these things from God? She didn't know what to do.

I invited her to come on an imaginary trip through time and space with me. The time was Good Friday, the place, Calvary. What did she see? She saw Jesus on the cross. What was happening? People were nailing him to the cross. What did he say? He asked his heavenly Father to forgive them because they didn't know what they were doing. How was that like her life? Maybe her father didn't know what he was doing to his children either. What else was Jesus doing? He was suffering and dying on the cross. Why was he doing that? He was winning forgiveness for the world. Whom did Jesus forgive? He forgave her. Whom else did he forgive? He also forgave her father. Why did Jesus forgive her? Because he wanted to forgive her. Why did Jesus forgive her father? Because he wanted to forgive her father.

How were her actions different from Jesus'? She didn't want to forgive her father. What reason had she discovered why she should forgive her father? Jesus already forgave him. What did that show her? She had no choice. She had to forgive her father. How did that make her feel? She didn't like it because she didn't want to forgive him.

What had her father done to her that was worse than what she was doing to her father? Nothing. What had her father done that was worse than what she was doing by withholding a gift Jesus already died to win? Nothing.

What was she doing to herself by carrying this grudge against her father? She was destroying her family life, depressing herself, spending her time doing the opposite of what she wanted to be doing for and with her family. Was her way of handling the problem working? Not at all.

How did Jesus' way of handling the problem work? It took all the sins of the world away. What was left for her to forgive now that Jesus already forgave everything and everyone? Nothing. What made it hard for her to forgive her father? She couldn't accept forgiveness for herself. What kept her from seeing God's forgiveness for herself? Her deep resentment. What had her father done to hurt her? He had neglected her. What happened to that sin? Jesus took it away. Now what was keeping her from forgiving her father? Nothing. What was keeping her from being forgiven herself? Nothing. Why was nothing hindering any of this? Jesus took it all away. What's left unforgiven? Nothing. What was left for her to carry? Nothing. What difference would that make? She could spend her time working with her family instead of against them.

How would she know this was happening? The attitude she had toward her family would be different. Was her attitude different? Yes. What would she do to keep it that way? She would keep going back to the cross to remember what Jesus did for her and for everyone else. How long would she need to do that? For the rest of her life. Would it be worth it to expend that effort? Yes. Why? Because it was too hard on her and on everyone else not to do it. She had carried her grudge long enough and she didn't want to carry it again.

One lady, Vicki, had continuing problems with her husband and with one of her children. She thought her husband was unconcerned about her oldest daughter's teen years, while he thought she was too busy butting into them. The question was one of control. How much control should the parents have, and whose responsibility should it be? Vicki felt unsupported by her husband, and her husband felt the demands Vicki was making were unreasonable. Their daughter felt the demands of her mother were unreasonable too. The primary concern at this point was the relationship between Vicki and her husband. Vicki's way of handling things was to try to get away from them. She would go for walks or long rides in the car. At times she even felt suicidal.

One time in particular Vicki felt extremely low and deserted by her husband. What would she do about that feeling? She felt like running away. How would that help? It wouldn't. How would she get away from these feelings for good? She could kill herself. What would that accomplish? She would be out of their way for good. How did she know they wanted her out of the way? That's the way she felt. Had she asked whether they wanted her out of the way? No. Why had she not asked this important question? She was afraid of the answer. What was she afraid the answer would be? She was afraid they would say yes. Why did that frighten her? She was afraid the truth she feared would come out. Why would it be worse to hear it from them than to believe it herself? It couldn't be any worse than it already was.

What could she do to handle the situation differently? She could ask them for their love. She could tell them, particularly her husband, that she needed him. What would he do? He would either let her down or give her what she really needed, namely, his love and support. Was she willing to risk this test? Yes, but she was afraid.

What could she do about those fears? She could pray about them. What answer did she want God to give? She wanted him to move her husband to accept her unconditionally. What if her husband failed? She would be devastated. Would her devastation be worse than what she was already feeling? No.

Where would she be able to find unconditional love? At the cross. Could her husband show the perfect love Jesus had shown unconditionally at the cross? No. Why not? He was a sinner. And what about her? She was a sinner too. Could she forgive her husband if he failed? Yes. Why? Because Jesus already did. Could she find forgiveness herself for feeling devastated? Yes. Why? Because Jesus forgave her. She realized too that she was showing more concern for herself than for her husband, her daughter and even for Jesus.

What was the worst thing that could happen? Her husband would disappoint her. What was the best thing that could happen? Her husband would surprise her. How would either situation change what Jesus did for her? It wouldn't. Where would she find her strength to stay and face the possibilities instead of running away from them? She would find them at the cross. How would she know whether Jesus had provided her the strength she needed? She would talk to her husband. Would she do it? Yes.

She did and she was not disappointed. She was more afraid to be loved than she was afraid not to be loved. Her husband was only waiting to find a way to express his love, but she would not allow it. Learning about Jesus' unconditional love took care of the problem.

These examples, as pedantic as they may seem, show the pains we must take to deal with the problems people have. We have the gospel, the good news of God's completed work in Christ. But sometimes we also have to go through a tedious process to make people aware of the gospel. We know people will, by nature, deal with their problems through an involved process of their own works. Sometimes other counselors, including some Christians, encourage an even more legalistic process for dealing with problems. Only those who are fully equipped with the gospel of free and faithful grace, the declaration of justification, and the doctrine of redemption that gives it its basis, are truly equipped for the work.

But having the equipment is not enough. We must use the equipment God has provided for us. We have no magical formulas and no quick cures. We may have been to the cross hundreds of times ourselves and with our people, but we know that the trip is necessary repeatedly, daily, weekly, yearly. One lady told me recently, "The first time I took that trip it was really hard. I didn't want to do it. I didn't want to think forgiveness would help. I was doing just fine working it out by myself. Then I asked myself, if I'm doing such a good job dealing with it myself, why am I in a pastor's office asking for help? I knew I had to take that trip as hard as it might be. Now it is easier to do it, but it's still necessary. I forget too easily."

We already know how easy it is for our people to forget how important that trip is. We can't forget the need to take them on the trip, no matter how often we've been to Calvary with them before. The quick solution would seem to be simply to say, "Jesus forgave you." Most of the time that is not enough. That statement will not shorten the amount of time we spend counseling with people to obtain resolution. Taking the trip to Calvary will shorten the time we spend counseling, however, because people will be working through the process to see how resolution became a reality. Their sin will be at the cross and they will know it. That is resolution.

That assurance of personal and particular forgiveness is what Jesus wanted to impress on his people when he gave them the "Visible Word" in the Sacrament of the Altar, saying, "This is given and shed for you for the remission of sins." My experience is that the trip to the cross produces in six weeks or less with one hour a week, what months and years of counseling and medication have not otherwise been able to accomplish. Everything after that is usually maintenance for the resolution the person has already experienced. In other words, in the gospel of justification supported by the gospel of redemption in the blood of Christ, we have a tool that works and works fast. God's declaration was made in a moment when Christ died and was affirmed when Christ rose again. The process started in eternity and ends in eternity.

Our people need to know where they stand with God. They are part of the process as long as God isn't yet finished with them. Justification states that fact. Redemption tells them how they got there. Sanctification is the process of living as God's people after we know we are God's people. When we spend the time to tell them how they got there, they will understand better that nothing they could do can get them the peace Christ already earned.

CHAPTER NINE
EXAMPLES OF HIDDEN GUILT THAT HINDER RESOLUTION

We have seen examples of guilt hidden beneath the surface of a problem. Whether dealing with depression, stress, anxiety, perhaps even physical symptoms, a particular sin or guilt may be the root of the problem. The hidden guilt we are addressing in this chapter takes an important turn. At times some hidden guilt keeps people from giving the help they should give other troubled people.

Unresolved guilt in the lives of "victims" can disable them from providing the direction they need to confront such things as children's behavior problems, problems with adoptive children, marriage problems, alcohol and substance abuse, and suicide. These are all serious problems that deserve special attention. We will be considering the "guilt trip" we hear so much about. This list of problems caused by people who take guilt trips is by no means exhaustive, but in all these problems we can find examples of people who didn't give the help they could have been giving because something else in their own lives kept them from giving it. As a result, resolution both for the troubled person and the guilt-ridden helper didn't occur.

For years, perhaps centuries, we have heard about the influence of the home on the lives of children. The Bible is filled with examples of the importance of training a child in the home for his future life away from home. In some cases in our modern society, parents are held financially and morally responsible for the acts of their children where destruction of property, physical harm or loss of life is concerned. Such actions have usually become necessary because of a total lack of concern and responsibility on the part of some parents. The opposite is also true. Some parents try to take total responsibility for the actions of their children. Those who take the responsibility so seriously that they bear the guilt for virtually everything their children do are the people we are talking about.

Matthew was a behavior problem in his fifth grade class in a Lutheran elementary school. His grades were low and getting lower. He was constantly taunting other children, sometimes to the point of starting fights he could usually win because of his size. Matthew was a bully. He was a discipline problem to his teacher and very uncooperative at home. His mother was raising him alone because her husband had deserted her several years earlier. No doubt that fact had an important influence on Matthew's life, but it had even more impact on his mother.

Matthew's mother not only felt responsible for Matthew's behavior, she carried a great burden of guilt because of her husband's desertion. If she had been a better wife, perhaps her husband would not have left, perhaps her son wouldn't be experiencing the difficulties he was having. In short, everything Matthew did was her fault.

His mother was incapable of addressing Matthew's responsibilities for his own actions. She had never addressed her own feelings of guilt.

To deal with this difficult matter, Matthew's mother,
Carolyn, had to come to grips with her own feelings.
Asking how she was responsible for her husband's desertion was fruitless. She had been asked that question
dozens of times before. She never gave adequate answers,
but all the rationalizations of other people did nothing to
help her resolve the problem. Before anything could be
done for Matthew and his situation, Carolyn had to work
out her feelings of guilt.

As we began our work we agreed hypothetically that
Carolyn was responsible for the breakup of her marriage.
She listed several thoughts on the subject. She wasn't
attentive enough. She took her career too seriously. She
did not respond to his needs as well as she could have. At
times he seemed to demand too much from her. In retro-
spect, however, she did not believe his demands were as
unreasonable as she thought they were at the time.

Whether any or all of these things were true or not is
not the issue. The point is that they were all real to
Carolyn. Whether her husband would have stayed with
her instead of leaving for another woman is also imma-
terial. Carolyn believed everything was her fault and no
one could successfully disagree with her. So, I agreed with
her. Everything was her fault.

What was she going to do about it now? She knew she
could not get her husband back. She could not even speak
to him to apologize. He was gone. The matter had to be
resolved within her own mind and heart. She realized she
was not acting in her son's best interests by allowing him
to misbehave so she could blame herself for his actions.
Carolyn had chosen a special way of paying for her sins.
The more her son misbehaved, the more guilty she felt,

the more she was punishing herself for the guilt she was already feeling. In a strange and misguided way all that, at least, made it possible for her to cope with her situation.

The only way to deal with Carolyn's problem was for her to take her own personal trip to the cross to get rid of the guilt she felt over what had happened in her marriage. Only then could she understand that she was also harming her son by failing to discipline him in love for his own benefit. Everything she had been doing was intended to benefit her, not her son. She realized how selfish she had been. She realized that Matthew's problem was his ability to sense her guilt and play on it. He could get away with anything because his mother always took responsibility for his actions. All that changed when Christ resolved Carolyn's guilt at the cross where he paid for the guilt she imagined and the guilt that was real. Matthew then began to see the love his mother had for him. He had only been seeing her take care of herself before.

The same process may occur when adoptive parents discipline their adopted children. Rather than sensing guilt, some adoptive parents fear the loss of their children's affection. Ironically, the way some of these parents show this love is not loving at all according to God's definition. Undisciplined behavior, emphasis on material things to display love, allowing children to decide how they want love to be shown is not love at all.

One family with adoptive children considered placing a young teenage daughter in a psychiatric unit for behavioral adjustment. Her behavior was such that no one could stand to be with her. Her psychiatrist suggested allowing her more freedom than she already had. That only made matters worse. The idea of two or three months of behavioral training looked all the more essential. The adoptive mother came to ask whether something else could be done. I asked whether she had tried to be more strict instead of more lenient. She said that both she and her husband had tried that and the results were temporary improvements. I asked whether that method seemed to work better than the psychiatrist's suggestion. It did.

Both father and mother met with me and we talked about the possibility of finding more and new ways of restricting their daughter for the purpose of showing her the limitations and boundaries by which her life would be ordered. We talked about the possibility of temporary setbacks and new attempts to break free that the daughter might, or probably would, try.

Both parents agreed they were willing to try this in lieu of psychiatric treatment on an inpatient basis, although the forty to sixty thousand dollars the treatment would have cost was not an issue. We agreed that *they* as much as their daughter needed treatment, or rather, education to cope with the problem. They would not receive the benefit of that education if someone else were teaching the child to behave instead of them. In addition, they considered the possibility that their daughter might actually learn new ways to misbehave if she associated daily with other children who had the same problems, or perhaps even worse than she did.

These parents confronted the fact that their daughter's behavior was not the only problem. In addition to her behavior problems, they were afraid they would lose her affection, if they had not lost it already. They were afraid they would lose her respect, although they were sure most of that was already gone. Most of all, they were afraid they would lose her permanently. They had to confront their own fears before they could deal with their daughter's behavior.

The fears were resolved when they realized that their daughter responded favorably when they expressed their concern for her and her well-being with tighter control.

More than that, they showed her a disciplined and directed love, rather than a love that allowed license and freedom to a child who was too young and immature to handle it.

Their daughter had exhibited unbridled anger. That anger had displayed itself in almost all her relationships with others, especially her parents. That anger had been her psychiatrist's primary concern. Nothing was done, however, to identify the source of the anger. The results showed that she had really been angry with herself for not being able to cope with all the new experiences placed before her as a child growing up. When her parents better understood the love God provides, their daughter began to understand it better too.

Hidden guilt can also play a large part in the cases of abused children, wives or husbands. On the surface a person who has been abused may sound angry and defensive, but often, not far below the surface is, "I feel so guilty." It may seem like a strange statement under the circumstances, but it is one that cannot be ignored.

Seemingly endless sources of material and help are available today on the subject of abuse. Statistics on backgrounds of abusers, habits of the abused, consequences of abuse are easy to find. Increased awareness has led to the establishment of hotlines for child and adult abuse. Authorities are much more ready to deal with the problem quickly and seriously. Today the police, schools, doctors, hospitals and help centers are equipped and also legally bound, to report abuse to specially equipped agencies, with sufficient authority, if necessary, to remove the abused person from the scene of the abuse.

Our concern here is not with the abuser and what prompts him or her to abuse another human being. Our concern is more for the reasons children or wives or husbands allow themselves to be abused, often to the point of serious personal injury and perhaps even death. Why should it be, for example, that a wife will allow herself to be abused and only attempt to stop the behavior when someone else, perhaps a child, is in danger of being hurt too? Why would she call the police for help and then interfere when the police do their job to protect her from her husband? Why should police tell us that domestic problems are probably the most dangerous problems to deal with?

One often sees children defending an abusive parent while condemning the one innocent of the offense. Likewise wives and husbands seem inclined to return for more abuse instead of protecting themselves from it.

In a book, *Why Battered Women Kill*, by Angela Browne, one might expect the answer to be obvious. You would expect that these women finally kill their husbands because they have been driven to it by constant abuse, and have finally decided to fight back in the only way they could. The statistics are quite to the contrary. The overwhelming reason for murder was not that these women were unable to tolerate what was happening to them. In the majority of cases, fear for harm to the children was the motive for murder. In other words, these women did not fight back until the safety and lives of their children were at stake. Their concern was not for themselves.

This prompts some interesting questions. What happens if the couple has no children? What happens if the safety of the children is not a factor? Why would a woman go back for more of the same abuse when a track record of abuse has already been established? Why do so few of these women bother to get to know their spouse before marriage, even to the point of failing to realize that several marriages have already ended in divorce, or a criminal record of violence has already been established, or the spouse is a known alcoholic or drug abuser?

One of the common answers the book provides for these questions is that most of these women live in the hope that the behavior will change. Usually the abuser deeply regrets the actions after they have taken place. Another possibility is that some women expect their husbands to abuse them. They actually feel they deserve abuse. Only when they can see abuse threatening another person are they able to see the behavior as inappropriate and unacceptable. While the wife may believe she deserves the abuse, the child does not deserve it. Then the wife fights back.

These possibilities lead to more interesting and important questions. Why would someone believe he or she deserves this kind of treatment? Does a child only defend an abusive parent because he or she is afraid of more of the same treatment? Or has the child even come to expect his parent to show love this way? Much more study will be done on this important problem as it receives increasing attention. We can only hope that those working in this field will not fail to examine the importance of hidden guilt in the lives of those being abused. Moreover, as Christian counselors, we must keep in mind that we cannot expect the secular community to involve itself with providing God's answer to a hidden guilt problem. Addressing guilt and resolving it is clearly in our area of concern and training.

Alcoholism and substance abuse also provide examples of hidden guilt at work, not only in the substance abuser, but especially in those around the abuser. Because of the increase in media exposure, we are becoming more aware of the symptoms of adolescent and adult substance abuse. In spite of this, parents are still shocked to find an alcohol or drug problem in the lives of their own children. Many parents are not ready to confront it. Several reasons for this neglect have been suggested. Perhaps parents of substance abusers are substance abusers themselves and actually indirectly encourage this behavior in their children. One public service television commercial shows a father who is angry to find his son with drugs and paraphernalia. He asks where the son learned about this. His son responds, "From you, Dad, from you." That response may keep a father from doing anything to help his son. Knowingly or unknowingly, those around a substance abuser may actually enable more substance abuse.

We can make excuses to explain why people might not be willing or able to see a problem and deal with it. We may say the process into drug abuse is too slow to be noticeable. Some parents may want to think this is only one of those experiences children need to have as part of growing up. Somewhere, however, we must acknowledge the serious possibility that guilt on the part of the enabler is keeping him or her from intervening to help stop the substance abuse.

What is true in the relationship between parents and children is also true in the relationship between adults themselves. The same kind of hidden guilt may keep a spouse from doing something to stop the substance abuse. People must be taught and encouraged to intervene. Many substance abuse centers are equipped to provide this teaching and encouragement.

Substance abuse centers have found that one of the more effective tools for addressing substance abuse is "the intervention." In an intervention, those who are closest to the abuser gather for the purpose of confronting the problem. The abuser does not know the intervention will take place. As many as possible who have some influence on the abuser meet for a common purpose. The intervention is designed to express as forcefully as possible how the abuse has affected each of those involved in the intervention. The intervention is not used to tell the abuser what he or she is doing to himself or herself.

Usually the intervention is done through a prearranged meeting, with the interventionists arriving equipped with letters for each to read to the person. Interventions present only two options. Either the abuser will get help, or he or she will no longer be a part of the lives of the interventionists. An employer may fire the abuser. A wife may force an alcoholic husband to leave the house. Visitation rights may be denied. Whatever anyone thinks will have an impact on the abuser is fair game for an intervention. In the meantime, everything necessary to obtain help, including packed bags, are part of the intervention. The abuser must choose whether to take the bag to a rehabilitation program or somewhere away from the lives of all concerned.

One reason why an intervention is more successful than other forms of confrontation is that confrontation is so difficult for only one individual to do. The power seems to be in the numbers. Even at that, establishing an intervention can be very difficult. While fear may be a primary factor, guilt is also present in many cases. This guilt may come in the form of, "What did I do to drive him to drink this way?" The guilt may also show as, "What will happen if she won't listen to me and get help, and just drinks more? How will I feel if I do this to her?" Those questions are sufficient to cause people to allow substance abusers to drive, to continue to drink, to destroy their brains and their whole bodies, even to cause death for the abuser or someone else. The guilt some people already feel keeps them from doing the very things that may help. It is guilt that, once again, we are equipped to address.

In one instance I was asked to confront an alcoholic woman with her abuse. Her husband carried the guilt of having moved to a location where his wife did not want to move. He believed his insistence on that move was responsible for her alcoholism. In that new location she found it difficult to make friends, she spent too much time alone, and she probably would not have become an alcoholic if he had done what she wanted him to do.

I had to ask this man how far he was willing to go to confront this problem. He was willing to put her into a program for rehabilitation and pay the ten thousand dollars it cost at that time. He was willing to have his children join in helping her confront the problem and deal with it. The woman herself was willing to undergo a screening for alcoholism and admit herself to the program. Her husband was extremely happy about this although he was still sorry he had done so much to upset her life.

An hour before she left the treatment facility on completion of her program she said, "As long as I don't have to suffer with all the aches and pains, I won't have any trouble staying off the liquor." In a word, the woman was promising to drink as soon as she got home. She did and two days later she was back in the hospital. Again her husband felt guilty.

The husband in this example had nothing to do with the alcohol problems his wife experienced, and yet he blamed himself for them. When they recurred he blamed himself again. The real problem was, however, that he was providing his wife with an excuse for her drinking. His own guilt was her most convenient tool. She would not improve until he was willing to reject the blame she was placing on him. The only way he could do that was to resolve his guilt at the cross and find his own peace with himself and God. When he found resolution at the cross, he was able to show love in the stern and demanding way his wife's sin demanded. Then serious work could begin to stop the drinking for good.

Once people have been able to deal with their own feelings of guilt and responsibility, they are equipped to take measures to put an end to the drinking or substance abuse of others in their family. Some have gone so far as to fire employees of long standing, not only because of failure to do the job expected of them, but as an indication of what these people were doing to themselves and others. Some have refused, even to the point of taking away car keys, to allow someone else to drive. Some have informed the police that a person was driving drunk in a car of a certain type with a particular license number on a particular road. All these things and many more harsh, but necessary, measures have been taken, when people have been able to deal with their own feelings of guilt and responsibility, and actually begin to love the abuser more than they love themselves.

This would be an appropriate place to examine what we have really been talking about all along, the so-called guilt trip. A guilt trip, in the minds of most people, is a feeling of guilt over the actions of another. Some people seem to be experts at putting others on guilt trips, while others are experts at taking the guilt trips handed out. Why should this exist? What can we do about it?

The primary reason one person would want to "lay a guilt trip" on another is that the person does not want to face responsibility for his or her own actions. If you can blame someone else for the problem, the feeling and the consequences, then you don't have to bear that responsibility yourself. In almost every instance I have worked with, I have found an underlying inability to accept responsibility for actions. While others might rationalize their actions or try to forget their actions, these people blame other people for their problems.

One lady suffered from depression for at least sixty years of her life. She had seen every psychiatrist available.

More than thirty years earlier she had received electroconvulsive treatments, a treatment that to this day some consider dangerous and unpredictable. This lady's method for dealing with her problem was to blame other people—her mother, her father, her sister, her brothers, her children, her friends, anyone—for making her feel the way she did. She was an expert, albeit a psychotic expert, at handing out guilt trips. They didn't show her enough attention, didn't get her the things she needed, didn't love her the way she needed to be loved. The list of the failures of other people was endless. Small inconveniences could ruin her whole week. The saddest part was that she loved being inconvenienced so she would have some failure to blame on other people.

Ironically, or perhaps predictably, her sister was an expert at taking guilt trips. Every time she was blamed for something, she accepted the blame. She felt bad. She was apologetic. She would offer all kinds of suggestions for ways to make up for the supposed wrong. Although she knew she was not responsible for her sister's miserable condition, had done nothing to cause it and everything she could to alleviate it, she still was always ready to take another guilt trip. Imagine the encouragement that action provided for her sister to do more of the same thing.

Both of those tendencies are difficult if not impossible to break after sixty or more years of practice. But the root problem was really the same in both cases. Neither of these two sisters had ever realized forgiveness for herself. If the one had learned God's forgiveness through an understanding of Christ's redemption, she would have had no need to try to shift her guilt anywhere but to the cross. If her sister, on the other hand, had learned Christ's forgiveness through an understanding of Christ's redemptive work, she would not have had to carry a load Christ already carried.

Guilt trips are a part of the lives of most of us whether we give them, take them or watch them happening to others. This alone can show us more effectively than many other indications, that people do go through processes of trying to get rid of guilt. They either shift it somewhere else or they punish themselves needlessly. If our people, then, whom we see on a daily basis, are going to all this trouble to deal with their guilt, shouldn't we work extra hard to take them on a trip to the cross to find the truth and resolution? Everything else is a lie that only inflicts more pain.

Sometimes doing what people need instead of what they want does not make one feel good about oneself. But it is love for Christ and others, not for ourselves, that should motivate our actions as Scripture-guided Christians. When Christ removes our guilt he leaves his love in its place. That love, in turn, motivates Christian discipline. In our counseling and in all our activities we must ask ourselves and our people whether we are showing Christian love as the Scripture directs us to show it, or are we just doing what makes us feel good about ourselves?

Here again we have the source for resolution at the cross. Jesus did not enjoy what he experienced there. The agony of hell he suffered was willingly accepted because of his concern for the world he came to save. Regardless of the personal cost he worked to win full and free forgiveness for everyone. His completed work left a perfect model for everyone to follow.

When we follow his example we find solutions to our problems. When we don't follow it the problems accumulate beyond measure. We and our people are left trying to figure out what to do with a load of guilt. Jesus already provided one and only one place to put it. If we are not putting it at the cross, we are preventing Christ from serving us with the redemptive work he already completed. That will not only harm us, but it may also cause us to fail to provide others with the peace Christ won. We will not provide the mirror and the direction of the law because it would hurt us to do that. We will not provide the assurance of forgiveness because we will be too busy protecting ourselves from any further hurt we might already be feeling.

Jesus talked about recognizing a plank in our own eye before we can adequately see to help someone else remove a speck. Jesus removed the plank so we can see clearly. We need to see clearly enough, through the forgiveness we have experienced, to share that forgiveness and remove the speck from someone else's eye. Jesus was talking about the very kinds of situations we have presented as examples in this chapter. His purpose was to convict self-righteous people. Carrying guilt needlessly is just as misdirected as pretending guilt doesn't exist. We are not likely to give others the help they need if we have not recognized our own need for help, and found resolution at the cross of Christ. But when Christ again shows us the blessing of his cross, the only fitting response is to share it with someone else who needs it.

EXAMPLES OF EMOTIONAL AND MENTAL PROBLEMS THAT HINDER RESOLUTION

A study of mental, emotional and personality disorders is far beyond the scope of this book. The treatment of those disorders within professional circles is beyond the competence of the writer. Nevertheless, mental, emotional and personality disorders occur within the confines of the Christian congregation. In fact, my experience has been that in almost any disorder, marriage problem, alcohol problem or the like, where national statistics exist, the rate of occurrence will be virtually the same in a congregation of a thousand members as it is nationally. The same probably holds true in much smaller congregations, and most certainly does in much larger ones.

If this is true, we have our work cut out for us. The comfort lies in the tools we have to do the work, and in the power of God at work through those tools. Those tools can help also where mental, emotional and personality disorders exist.

We should state at this point that our concern here is not with organic disorders causing such problems. Mental retardation, brain damage, brain tumors and seizures, chemical and metabolic disorders are issues that demand medical or other specialized attention. We are not faith healers. We know God has provided medical knowledge to serve his purposes. Nevertheless, in all of these instances we also have spiritual work to do and are equipped to do it. We do that spiritual work whenever our people are hospitalized. We can also present the beauty and the comfort of the gospel in its simplicity to people who are mentally retarded. Many other examples could be cited. A mutual respect between the pastor and the medical profession is important as we work for the successful resolution God provides. The doctor has his or her work to do, and we have ours. The work is different, but all of it is important.

One of the most common disorders among our people, as among the general population, is panic, or anxiety attacks, that may lead to agoraphobia. Literally, agoraphobia is the fear of the marketplace. People who suffer from this disorder often become completely housebound. They cannot stand to be outside their homes except for extremely short periods of time, if at all. They may become claustrophobic, afraid of being trapped in certain places or even in crowds. Agoraphobia manifests itself within the circles of the church because these people will not or cannot come to church. Some of them are on our delinquent lists, but we often ignore the possibility that agoraphobia is the problem.

One such example was Fred, a middle-aged man. He never held a job because as long as his parents could remember he always wanted to be at home. The family was very concerned about his spiritual life, although he spent a great deal of time in personal Bible study. Some

Christians might have even envied him the time he was able to spend with it because of his agoraphobia. The family seemed to experience some success with a man at a Christian counseling center. Once a week Fred would go with his parents to his session, some ten miles from home, and the family would spend $35 for the forty-five minute visit. Fred seemed to be doing better because he was more willing to work outside in the yard, and even did some odd jobs for the neighbor next door. The problem, as his parents saw it, was that it had taken three years to reach this point.

When the matter first came to my attention, the parents, new members of the congregation, came to talk about it. No one was even aware they had a son, much less a son at home. As we talked about the problem and the way it was being handled, I asked whether Fred might not be getting better just because he was forced once a week to leave the house. The parents seemed to think that was a reasonable possibility. Perhaps Fred had not really received any therapy at all. The drive to and from the session was his therapy, not what happened after he arrived at the counselor's office.

Still his parents and I shared the same concern: What about Fred's spiritual life? We had to find a way to meet him, to talk with him, to build confidence in him. That was no easy task. His parents asked if Fred would like to meet their pastor. He was unwilling. Just stopping by meant Fred would leave for his room immediately. Fred's problem was deep and years old. The only thing we knew for sure was that Fred was not really getting over his problem at all. The way he was being treated by his counselor was not the answer.

Fred's parents took an entirely different outlook on the kind of therapy their son was receiving. The improvement was not adequate, considering the amount of time and money involved. They realized the counseling was only hindering resolution of the problem, because, while they had thought they were doing something about it, they were only prolonging it. Fred was not getting better, and, more important, he was not getting the spiritual care his parents desired for him and that he desired himself.

When we did have a chance to meet and begin to talk, I told Fred frankly that I didn't know whether we could overcome his agoraphobia, but we could help him to be the most spiritually healthy agoraphobic God could make of him. He was willing to grow in his understanding of God's word, both law and gospel; and his agoraphobia diminished proportionately, though slowly. The day he is able to walk into church and sit through a service will be a day of joy, not only for Fred and his parents and me. I believe the angels of God will share in the rejoicing. Meanwhile, and although he may never be able to join the church service, he can share the means of grace with fellow Christians.

Perfectionism is another disorder that is very common among the population of our country. Some may not consider perfectionism a disorder, but the attention to details, the personal demands and, sometimes, the self-punishment fit into several categories in the American Psychiatric Association's, *DSM-III R, The Diagnostic and Statistical Manual for Mental Disorders, Third Edition-Revised.*

One lady, Amy, placed herself under so much stress by the unreasonable demands she made on herself that for almost three years she was virtually unable to live with herself or anyone else. She manufactured illnesses, talked for hours about her childhood and the abuse she supposedly suffered. At times she would have psychotic breaks that would leave her in a state of apparent unconsciousness, staring at the wall instead of finishing a sentence. At times these breaks would last more than two hours.

Indications were, however, that Amy had the ability to fake these psychotic breaks, and was only trying to instill fear and sympathy because she was under so much pressure. The real question she had to answer was where was all this pressure coming from?

Amy soon realized that no one was placing undue pressure on her. She was doing it all by herself. The best indication of this came when she said she would have a nervous breakdown if she had to bear anymore pressure than she was already bearing. I suggested she would not have a nervous breakdown. When she asked why, I told her that if she had enough control over the situation to threaten to have one, she had enough control over it to keep it from happening. Once again she was trying to give credence to the idea that others demanded perfection of her. Amy wanted some kind of gospel comfort for her situation. What she needed at that point was the law.

Amy had purposely placed herself in a position superior to God himself. While God demands perfection of people, Christ was the one who provided it. Christ provided it because people can't. What Amy was doing, in effect, was to say she should be able to do just as good a job of living as Christ himself. As a result she had no need for Christ. Her craving for the gospel was only a craving for sympathy. She had no intentions of trusting Christ to provide the perfection she could not give. She had no intention of repenting for expecting to obtain perfection. She had no intentions of letting God even be God. She had made a god out of herself.

When Amy realized her sin, she also realized her need for the Savior was entirely different from what she expected. She was looking for a Savior who would put his arms around her and pat her on the back for doing so much to serve him. What she found was a Savior who was willing to forgive her for not letting him save her from her imperfections, her sins.

Of all the emergencies people face, mental and emotional emergencies may be the most devastating. We have many more facilities and much better training to deal with medical emergencies than the others. At times of mental emergencies, pastors often find out that one of their members has been under psychiatric care for a considerable length of time. He finds out when the family calls and says someone in the family has "flipped out." The family does not expect the pastor to solve the problem as much as they expect him to know how to deal with it.

On one occasion, a young man appeared to be under the influence of drugs. A preliminary investigation by a doctor in a hospital without psychiatric facilities proved this was not the case. The young man, Greg, was released to his parents' care. By the next day Greg was threatening his father with a knife and was taken to a mental hospital in an ambulance and restraints. He spent two months in the facility and was eventually released with heavy doses of medication. The medical staff and the counseling staff did nothing to find Greg's root problem.

This case illustrates one of the basic tensions pastors are likely to see in these settings. In some cases strong disagreements exist between psychologists and psychiatrists. Psychiatrists are medical doctors whose primary tool is medication to control psychotic behavior. A psychologist is more likely to try to deal with the patient through some kind of conversational therapy. If a pastor has the resources available to make use of both psychologists and psychiatrists who work together as a team, he has a valuable resource. Without that cooperation, a pastor is likely to get caught up in the basic tensions between the two fields. This lack of cooperation and mutual respect can be damaging to the healing process.

In one instance, Shirley, a young mother, began to show schizophrenic tendencies. She could not sleep. Her mind constantly ran wild. She did not take care of her children or herself. Her dress was bizarre. Sometimes she walked all over town barefoot, giving flowers to people she met along the way. She accepted rides from several total strangers, and was in the process of carrying out some kind of imitation of the work the disciples of Jesus did when they went out to share the gospel without purse or an extra pair of shoes.

Shirley's first experience with a mental institution was in a nearby hospital. She was given medication to reduce her hyperactive behavior, another medication to control muscle tension caused by the first medication, and still another medication to control her mood swings. After two weeks she was released. Three months later she was in the same condition again. She hated taking her medication. She believed she was better and didn't need it. This is a common problem with people using psychiatric medications.

Shirley's second experience with a mental institution involved a three-month stay at a hospital where she had both medical and psychological assistance. She was not admitted as a schizophrenic because, in many circles, medication is the only means for dealing with schizophrenia. Instead, since a psychologist admitted her, she was admitted as a person with a schizotypal personality. This meant that she showed traits of schizophrenia, but suspicions existed of an underlying motive for her behavior. In other words, she could do something about the way she was acting.

Her psychologist was a devout Christian who graciously allowed me to participate in her therapy. He uncovered layer after layer of motivation for her behavior. During her time in the hospital, Shirley spent extensive time in psychiatric intensive care, meaning she was always in view of a staff member. She even slept in the hallway. She was dangerously suicidal. At one point she was so hostile her psychologist was frightened by her. Her eyes were piercing and full of hate. Her psychologist, a man with years of experience, refused to work with her any longer.

She was moved by ambulance to a state facility. She was immediately labeled schizophrenic and treated with various medications. When she was at her best she was like a zombie. When she didn't take her medication she vented hatred and bitterness.

After her release from the state institution her former psychiatrist agreed to resume her treatment. When her condition worsened again I asked for permission to meet with the doctor, Shirley and her husband. I had only one question. Was Shirley's condition something she could control or not? That had been the basic question when she was admitted to the hospital by her psychologist.

The answer we had received early in her treatment was a resounding yes, Shirley can control her behavior. Shirley can work herself into this condition where nothing but medication can get her out of it. Shirley can start something she can't stop. Her actions were much like those of people who deal with stress by getting ulcers. They start the problem emotionally (a psycho-somatic illness), but once they start it they will probably need a medical doctor and medication to stop it.

The answer of the psychiatrist was that he was not sure whether her actions were self-motivated or not. I had expected him to say she was self-motivated but that she needed medication to stop what she started. The tension between the medical and psychological communities was clear. Shirley was victimized by the indecision.

I felt betrayed by the doctor who had been working for three years under the assumption that Shirley's behavior was self-motivated. He did agree, however, that one way or another she had to control her behavior. By this time her husband was in danger of losing his job because of the constant need to tend to his wife. The children were spending most of their time with grandparents. People in town constantly received calls as Shirley tried to win sympathy. Ironically, she had a list of people she would call and a list she would not call. She would call those who sympathized with her. She would not call those who wouldn't. This seemed to bear out even more strongly that her actions were self-motivated. She knew where she could get support for what she wanted.

The first step to correcting this behavior was to do what had not been done for five years. In consultation with her and her husband, I told her to stop behaving the way she was behaving. We showed her that her behavior was not getting her the kind of attention she wanted. We let her know that if her behavior continued she would lose privileges.

For a period of time she was not allowed to use the phone. Within days her behavior changed completely. The doctor was able to reduce her medication. Her grandiose ideas about her abilities and talents diminished. Her anxiety diminished significantly. Her circles of confidants learned new ways of handling her when she began to show hostility toward her husband. Some thirty people received new understanding of Shirley's way of behaving and the symptoms of misbehavior. All evidence of suspicious action was immediately reported to me or to her husband, and we shared what we had learned. We dealt with it together, all three of us. Shirley always knew what we were doing. All her attempts at renewed motivation were met with stiff and immediate opposition.

This criterion explains the law approach to dealing with Shirley's problem. The gospel served a purpose that was far greater. Shirley began to realize that what she wanted was not nearly as important as what God wants. She could see the workings of his patience and love. Her understanding of Christ's love and patience enabled her to show her love in a way she had been unable to show it before. She got more out of sharing what Christ gave her than she did out of demanding what she wanted. Shirley has not been hospitalized since her last episode four years ago. She still needs medication and still has periods of ups and downs. She still tries motivating her behavior toward her own self-interests, but what she really wants and needs she only gets from Christ and those who help her stay close to him.

Psychosomatic illnesses fall into the category of emotional and personality disorders. Contrary to popular understanding, however, psychosomatic illnesses are not imagined. Psychosomatic illnesses are as real as gastric and duodenal ulcers, ulcerated bowels, respiratory ailments, pulmonary and heart diseases, spastic portions of the digestive tract, allergies and the like. Although genetic disorders alone can cause any or all of these things, many are at least aggravated by psychological problems. We heard before about Charles who tried to do God's work instead of being a workman for God. Many other psychological causes for similar problems could be cited.

One lady, Ellen, was hospitalized for chest pains. She was placed in the intensive care unit for tests and observation. No medical cause for her discomfort presented itself. She was moved from intensive care but remained in the hospital for further testing. I had a lengthy opportunity to talk with her while she was hospitalized. Her doctor was also a man both of us trusted and appreciated. In his work as a cardiologist, we have had numerous opportunities to discuss serious patient problems. We have come to respect each other highly.

I took the opportunity when I saw her doctor to suggest that in his medical evaluations he keep in mind that Ellen was hospitalized on the first anniversary of the week in between the death of her two sisters, who both died of cancer. The doctor said he suspected some sort of stress was the problem. For a year Ellen had not really dealt with the death of her sisters. Her friends were aware that she had learned to blot those thoughts out of her mind. The first anniversary made it impossible for her to do that, but her mind could not cope with the experience. As a result, her body reacted to her denial. The time had come for her to confront her grief and find the comfort only God could give her.

Much more could and should be said about grief and, perhaps, all the other kinds of mental, emotional and personality disorders that get in the way of resolution. Suffice it to say that all of these disorders can be frightening enough in themselves to keep us from looking beneath the presenting problem to the spiritual problem at the root of it, if there is one.

To complicate matters further, we have seen that often little agreement exists between professionals on how to handle certain problems. Medication, for example, has its place, a very important place. But we have more than enough proof that medication does nothing to settle the underlying anxiety or depression or whatever the cause might be. The medication may make a person feel better. It may make it easier for those around the troubled individual to cope with the problem. It may reduce the symptoms. But, as in Shirley's case, the medication can merely mask the real deep needs the individual insists on holding. In her case, even when she was under medication, one could perceive the same bitterness and hatred in a shabby disguise. Under those circumstances, medication may actually hinder resolution of the problem.

The widespread use of prescription medication shows how easy it is for doctors and for people to think a pill will make everything better. Elvis Presley, whether you are a fan or not, is a well-known example of a person who could not resolve an inner conflict with a whole drug store full of prescription medication. Too many people are following that example to the same end. Elvis Presley died at age 42 of the very thing he hoped would be his deliverance. Many have died much younger, many older. Over twenty-five years ago Karl Menninger in his book, *Whatever Became of Sin?*, spoke of valium as the only glue holding together a world coming apart.

One might be inclined to ask, "Whatever happened to grace and the gospel for resolution?"

CHAPTER ELEVEN
SOME TECHNIQUES FOR OBTAINING RESOLUTION

Every faithful Christian preacher knows he will never be able to add any power to the word of God by his preaching. No matter how forceful, dynamic or interesting the preaching might be, the power to save is in God's word. The same is true with counseling. No one can add any power from secular psychology, from particular gifts, from computerized testing, or from expensive therapy sessions that will produce a power equal to or even supplemental to the word of God. But just as a preacher will work at increasing his own effectiveness as a preacher, counselors can increase their own effectiveness as counselors. The end result is a more efficient presentation, a more focused presentation of the law and the gospel to produce resolution.

We can thank the secular and professional field for many "tricks of the trade." Basically we are talking about communication skills. The secular and professional fields of counseling have made great strides in improving upon communication, diagnostics, program outlines, record

120

keeping and other techniques for counseling. Many of these techniques have valuable applications for gospel resolution, just as the media can provide valuable avenues for the dissemination of the gospel.

We have a multitude of ways to obtain increased proficiency in counseling through the improvement of techniques. The means I have found most beneficial have been postgraduate courses in counseling techniques, participation in and observation of professional psychological and psychiatric work, reading and studying about abnormal psychology and behavior, and, of course, experience.

None of these means for increasing proficiency is particularly taxing or time-consuming. The only essential ingredient is the determination to find new and better ways to disseminate the same gospel we have always preached, for the purpose of helping a person resolve his problems in daily life. Without that commitment, no amount of increased proficiency will be of any value. What good would it do to be proficient at doing your work if you don't know what your work is?

I have chosen several techniques that have become important to me. The sources are many and varied and it would be impossible to give credit where credit is due. Suffice it to say I have learned to appreciate anyone, or any technique, that offers a way to present the gospel more effectively. I'm thankful for them all.

LISTENING

If someone calls your office to talk to you, that automatically puts you in the position of being a listener. As obvious as that may seem, it goes against the grain of many pastors and teachers. We are trained talkers. We are much better trained to talk than to listen. That fact alone causes a great many pastors to sense failure in their counseling ministries. If a counseling session lasts only thirty minutes, if counseling means one session and you're done, then the chances are you're not listening.

Nevertheless, many of us feel the responsibility to give quick and easy answers to any and all problems that come to us. For example, "Pastor, I'm troubled by my sin." "Member, your sin has been forgiven by Jesus. Believe it and don't sin again." With that method of counseling a pastor or teacher is likely to say counseling is not time-consuming and very few people in his congregation have many problems they need to talk to him about. Why should they want to talk to him if he doesn't listen any better than that?

To carry the matter further, a pastor may listen carefully as a member pours out his or her heart about a problem, but then he responds with a pat answer that would apply just as well to an alcoholic grandfather or a pregnant teen-ager. Pat answers give almost as much impression a coun-selor wasn't listening as not listening itself. It gives the impression that the individual problem isn't that impor-tant to the counselor.

One way to overcome listening problems like these is to become a more active listener. Asking questions will help you do so. For example, you might ask, "What did you mean by that?" Or, "Would you put that in different words so I can be sure I understand you?" You may choose to repeat what you heard and ask whether you heard correctly what the person meant. Usually such responses will encourage people to tell you more or perhaps even bring out a new thought. One time a person spoke for over forty-five minutes and I didn't understand the point of the problem. I simply told the gentleman I was sorry, but I didn't understand the point he was trying to make. He responded, "I think you hit the nail on the head, Pastor. I'm confused."

Listening takes concentrated effort. Listening involves more than keeping the mouth shut, it also involves keeping the mind open. On numerous occasions I have repeated the very words a person has spoken and put them together with other words spoken by the same person to point out a contradiction. People usually respond better when they are hearing their own words than someone else's. People are often amazed to find that they have really answered their own questions, solved their own problems, or, at least, identified their own problems, simply by hearing someone take their words and rearrange them in a more orderly way.

Listening sometimes involves watching people cry. This is difficult for some people. Crying is an indication someone is hurting, and we don't like to see other people hurt. But if you remember that the person came to you because he or she was hurting, you'll realize the tears are beneficial. They help you discover where the real problem lies. If a person can talk calmly for forty-five minutes and then begins to cry at the forty-sixth minute, the person has given you an indication that what he or she is talking about at minute forty-six is the crux of the problem.

Besides seeing tears as an indication of the real problem, common practice is to take careful note of the first thing a person says when the session begins. One lady who always came equipped with a notebook full of written dissertation began by saying, "I have a poor self-image." She continued by talking about how miserable she was in her marriage, and that continued for most of the session. I asked why she began by talking about her own self-image. She didn't know. Before long she was ready to admit that she felt guilt because perhaps her poor self-image had destroyed her marriage.

This example brings another important aspect of listening to mind. After listening to people talk for some time a counselor begins to notice some things that are conspicuous by their absence. One of those conspicuous absences is the willingness or ability to admit to a poor self-image. Most people who demonstrate a poor self-image don't necessarily talk about it. In some cases, in fact, a person who says he or she has a poor self-image is really telling you that you are supposed to say he or she is a pretty good person.

One man I spoke with had perhaps the worst image of himself of anyone I have ever met. He never spoke about self-image, he simply said over and over that he was worth nothing. He was incapable of understanding a poor self-image because his own opinion was already meaningless.

People who talk about their poor self-image have placed themselves in a position where their opinion of themselves is worth something at least to them. That is completely out of character for a person with a truly poor self-image. Listening can bring all this out so the real crux of the matter comes to light.

Substance abuse counselors often encounter the same phenomenon. If a man enters the office and says he is an alcoholic, the chances are he said that to close the subject to further conversation. "Look, I already told you I'm an alcoholic. I came to you because I want you to tell me what to do about my wife."

Another much more difficult and very important part of counseling technique is listening for, recognizing and interpreting encoded messages. Usually people are not even aware they are sending an encoded signal. An encoded message is an underlying message hidden in words that apply to the superficial conversation. For example, a lady may say, "I called before, but you weren't in. I've tried several times to get hold of you. I know how busy you are." The message probably means, "Why don't you ever have time for me? You have time for everyone else." Another common encoded statement is, "I don't want to burden you with my problems." This usually means one of two things. It could mean, "I don't want to talk to you," or it could mean, "I want to find out whether you care enough about me to listen to me instead of doing something else."

The most important kinds of encoded messages are suicidal threats buried within an otherwise trivial conversation. For example, two people may be talking about a ball game. One says, "That was a great game. I wonder whether the team will do that well tomorrow." The other responds, "Yeah, that was a great game all right. I've seen a lot of good games in my life. I don't know how many more I'll get to see. Tomorrow's game will probably be just as good as this one, but I'm not sure I'll be here to see it." That may only mean the person has other things to do and won't be able to watch the next day's game. It may mean he doesn't expect to be alive to see it. One statement alone is probably meaningless if it's buried in trivia. Four or five together is a suicide threat. Dr. Marvin Miller, a suicidologist in San Diego, lists twenty-nine encoded suicide messages that may be warning signs of a suicide threat. They are listed in the appendix.

One time a lady, Mrs. Burrows, called because she was very upset and wanted to talk. I went to her house. She had been canning all night. She had to get the canning done. Time was running out, and she didn't know how much more time she would have. I asked her whether she couldn't put some of it off till tomorrow. She couldn't. She didn't know whether she would be there to do it and this was something she could do to take care of her family even when she was gone. That was enough. My conscience forced me to contact her husband and daughter and make sure she had someone with her through the day. By that evening she was admitted to a psychiatric unit with a suicidal depression.

QUESTIONS

In counseling, questions serve two important purposes. Questions may be diagnostic or therapeutic. We ask questions to identify the problem, and we ask more questions to lead a person to resolution. Questions allow a person to talk about and explain the problem. Questions also allow the person to formulate verbally the answers to his own problems. Although the techniques for questioning can become complex, a few simple rules allow for more effectiveness.

Rule one: Most "Yes" or "No" questions are useless unless you want to establish a very basic case history or do most of the talking yourself. When you ask a question that can be answered with a yes or no, that's probably all you will get. Then it's up to you to figure out what to ask next. Your member will not give you much help along those lines.

Rule two: "Why" questions are also particularly unproductive. You may begin by saying, "Why did you come here today?" If the person feels a bit uneasy about being in your office for the first time, his response may be, "I don't know. I think I made a mistake by coming." A better way to begin might be, "What would you like to talk about?"

"Why" questions intended to identify a problem are also unrewarding. "Why do you feel the way you do?" "I don't know. That's what I want you to tell me." Questions that begin with "What," "When," "Where," "Who," "How" are all much more productive. Perhaps the following example of a questioning procedure might serve to illustrate diagnostic questioning.

A lady has come to discuss how bad she feels about the way her children are treating her. She doesn't know whether she's right to feel the way she does, but she doesn't like the feeling.

Pastor: What is the problem you're experiencing?

Ann: I came to talk about what my children are doing.

P: What are they doing?

A: They're treating me like dirt.

P: What do they do that makes you feel that way?

A: Either they don't pay any attention to me at all, or they make it very clear they don't want to be with me.

P: When did you first notice this?

A: About three months ago.

P: What happened in your children's lives three months ago?

A: Nothing special I can think of.

P: What happened in your life three months ago?

A: Nothing special, but my dog died.

P: How did you feel about that?

A: I felt much worse than I thought I would feel. I've felt so alone for the last two years since Brad, my husband, passed away.

P: How did Brad's death affect your children?

A: They had just as rough a time as I did with it.

P: How are they doing now?

A: Much better than I am.

P: What makes you think they're doing better than you are?

A: They have each other, but now I have no one, not even the old dog.

By now we know what the problem is. Ann's children are not treating her badly. They're not treating her any differently than they ever did. She is the one who doesn't think she fits into anyone's life. None of her children could do anything to replace either her dog or, more important, her husband. Still she wants them to take her back to the good old days when Dad was there and the kids were the kids. Now they have families of their own, and she resents it.

What holds true of diagnostic questioning also holds true of therapeutic questioning. The "Why" questions and the "Yes" and "No" questions are not very helpful. Our purpose and goal is always to seek resolution through the gospel. To illustrate therapeutic questioning we will continue the issue with Ann and her pastor:

P: What do you think is really bothering you? You haven't told me about anything your children are doing that's much different from the way they always acted.

A: I think my dog's death bothered me more than I thought it did.

P: In what way did the dog's death bother you?

A: I'm all alone now.

P: What makes you say you're all alone?

A: I can't help thinking that my husband is gone too.

P: What does your dog have to do with that?

A: Nothing.

P: What do your children have to do with that?

A: Nothing, except that they have each other and I have no one.

P: What do you mean you have no one?

A: I guess I mean I have no one the way I used to have Brad.

This brings us to a point in the questioning process known as the confrontation or revelation. In this case we have more of a confrontation. The pastor doesn't have to tell Ann anything she doesn't already know. He can merely organize her thoughts for her so she understands which way her anger, the real problem, is directed.

P: I think you put your finger on the real problem just now. You cared much more about Brad than you do about the children. That's natural and God-pleasing. Marriage is the closest of all human relationships. Your children can't compete with that relationship and commitment you had with Brad. The death of your dog only reminded you of what you said earlier. You're all alone now. That makes you angry, doesn't it, angry enough to take it out on your children?

P: Where is this anger coming from?

A: It's coming from deep inside me.

P: What have you been doing to deal with it?

A: I've been blaming the children for my anger.

P: What have your children done to deserve your anger?

A: Nothing.

P: What can they do to take your anger away?

129

A: Nothing.

P: With whom are you really angry?

A: I'm angry with myself for the way I feel.

P: What do you want to do with the anger inside you?

A: I guess I have to learn to control it better.

P: How do you intend to do that?

A: I'll pray for God to help me get over it.

P: How do you know God will help you do that?

A: He promised to hear my prayers.

P: How do you feel about going to God with this problem?

A: I'm not sure if he'll make all this go away. I guess I'm angry with him too. Maybe he's angry with me.

P: What makes you unsure?

A: I don't know whether God cares that much. If he did, why did he take Brad away from me in the first place?

P: That sounded like a pretty angry statement. Think again about your anger. Who really makes you angry?

A: God does. He took Brad. I never thought of it that way before.

P: How does it feel to know you are angry with God?

A: I feel terrible.

P: What would you like to do about the way you feel?

A: I'd like to tell him I'm sorry.

P: Go ahead and tell him you're sorry.

A: Lord, I'm sorry for the anger I've been feeling.

P: What else would you like to do?

A: I'd like to ask him to forgive me.

P: How can God forgive you for being angry with him?

A: I just hope he will, and he said he would.

Now it's time for the trip to the cross to resolve the matter.

P: How can you be sure of his forgiveness?

A: I know Jesus died to forgive me.

P: Come with me in your imagination to where Jesus died. Imagine the cross, the nails, the soldiers and everything. What is Jesus doing there?

A: He is dying.

P: Why is he dying?

A: To pay for sins.

P: Which sins is he paying for?

A: All of them.

P: What sin matters the most to you right now?

A: My anger with him and with myself.

P: Take a good look at those sins of yours. What do you see?

A: I see them at the cross.

P: What do you hear Jesus saying?

A: He said, "It is finished."

P: What does that mean to you?

A: It means he's done with my sins.

P: What does that mean you can do with them?

A: I am finished with them too.

P: Where is your anger?

A: At the cross.

P: Would you like to bring it back here to the office with you?

A: No.

P: Would you like to take it home with you and give it to your children?

A: No.

P: What would you like to do now?

A: I'd like to go home and be with my children and tell them how much they mean to me and how good God has been to all of us.

Of all the possible ways a similar conversation like this could go, of all the ways people might have struggled to rationalize, retaliate, hate, hurt or grieve, only the cross of Christ allows a person like Ann to depart in peace with the matter resolved. With simple questions and answers she figured that out for herself. The results are much more effective than giving her all the answers she already knew and might have expected her pastor simply to tell her.

The question and answer process accomplishes two important things. When diagnosing a problem, it allows a person the opportunity to explain the problem in detail. It prompts him or her to make a serious evaluation of what the root problem actually is. All too often we can easily draw those conclusions for our people. That leaves us open to being wrong and working to resolve the wrong thing. Furthermore, drawing conclusions for people leaves the impression that we and not they will do whatever must be done to accomplish resolution. When our people think through both the diagnosis and the therapy by carefully directed questions, they themselves get involved in seeking and discovering the resolution in their relationship with God.

VARIOUS TECHNIQUES USED IN COUNSELING

Some techniques used in counseling and psychotherapy have value in our counseling to a greater or lesser degree. Books are available to study any and all of them to the extent that a pastor or teacher would consider them valuable. I am listing a few of them to allow the reader to consider their usefulness in the ministry.

The family constellation, that is, the family tree and where an individual fits into it, is receiving widespread attention. It has its roots in the psychotherapy of Alfred Adler and has recently been popularized by Kevin Leman. Books like Leman's, *The Birth Order Book*, have popularized the subject. Firstborn children act in a predictable way. Second children act in a particular way. The baby in the family acts in yet another way. The subject can be studied in as much complexity as one wishes.

Personally I have not found the study of the family constellation to be as helpful as some might expect. The study seems to have more value in predicting the way a person will handle a situation than it does in aiding resolution. Without overstating the case, the popularity of the family constellation seems to be more interesting to the people themselves than it is beneficial to them, trying to help them work out problems. Nevertheless others may strongly disagree with that conclusion and have possibly found the study to be helpful in diagnosing problems.

This brings up an important point we should not overlook when we consider our place as Christian counselors. One advantage we have that even the best workers in the secular and professional fields do not have is a firsthand knowledge of our people. Perhaps this is one reason why a study of the family constellation is not as helpful to us as it might be to others. While this study might help others get to know the people they are trying to help, we already know them, sometimes on a personal level with special insight. We have seen them in classes, at meetings, with others, serving the church, not serving the church, and so forth. Other counselors our people might seek for help do not have the advantage of those observations.

In some cases I have encouraged people to obtain diagnostic testing from a psychologist with the facilities to offer it. Many psychological tests are now computerized. A person can spend thirty minutes to three hours pushing buttons on a computer and within minutes after completion, a complete profile of personality, including charts, graphs, a verbal evaluation and a suggested course of treatment, follows. In some instances these tests can be administered without a computer and then mailed in for computer analysis. This is convenient when work sheets can be used in the counselor's office or at home, and then mailed to a testing firm for processing.

Two important items are necessary to make use of this kind of testing. First, a release of information from the person undergoing the test, preferably on a signed form, is necessary to allow the psychologist to do the testing and to share the results with the pastor. In addition, a close working relationship with a psychologist who has these instruments and will share and assist in interpreting the results is essential.

Many psychologists do not wish to share this kind of information with someone else who is doing the counseling. Although he is paid for his testing services, he would also like to control the therapy. Another reason for hesitation is a psychologist's reluctance to share the information for fear that the pastor, teacher or counselor will not know how to deal with it, will not understand it and will not use it appropriately. Only a close and, perhaps, personal relationship of respect and trust between counselor and psychologist will overcome these barriers. When they are overcome, some valuable insights and measurements are available.

At one time I considered this testing to be very helpful, if not essential, for doing intensive work. As time went on I began to notice the tests were providing information I already knew or suspected. For that reason I have not used these resources as often as I once did. These tests are expensive and often time-consuming. We should have a definite reason for requesting our members to use them.

One good reason to use the tests is to verify a suspicion. As in the case of Jennifer, the anorexic alcoholic mentioned previously, two possibilities existed. Either the person was resisting treatment or she had already suffered brain damage. The course of treatment would have been different depending on the results of testing, both psychological and medical. In that case, however, the suspicions, or "gut feelings," about resistance were correct. The testing would have merely substantiated them.

One more factor that I have found particularly helpful about the personality inventory or other psychological tests is that most of the verbal evaluations begin with a statement suggesting whether the person has told the truth or lied in taking the test. If a test suggests a person lied about certain things, a pastor or teacher can be more aware of the person's attempts to give him the answer he wants to hear, instead of the truth about how he or she actually feels.

Obviously a relationship of working confidence with a psychologist who has instruments like these is helpful. In my experience, the best psychologists to consult with are those who are extremely busy in their practices. They will be more likely to share information and allow you to do the counseling because they cannot afford the time, and do not need to add more clients to fill their schedules. Besides, these people are probably busy because they are good at what they do. They have more valuable information to share, and are not as reluctant as others might be to share it.

While we might not personally agree with their theology, many psychologists will allow pastors or teachers to share in therapy sessions. Those I have worked with have been respectful of my work, and often have been more careful than I would have been to say, "That's your pastor's field. You should take up that subject with him." That kind of relationship is a real gift of God. It presents itself most often when we remember we are pastors and not amateur psychologists. If we do not try to do their work, they will likely not try to do ours. If we respect their profession, they are likely to respect ours.

Another sometimes helpful item in the counseling technique "bag of tricks," is the early recollection. You simply ask people what is the earliest memory in their life. The anorexic and alcoholic lady mentioned earlier, remembered shaking her crib when she was two years old, but no one came. That was a picture of nearly everything in her life. Most of what she did was a form of shaking her crib to get people to pay attention to her and give her what she wanted. Her early recollection was also the earliest I have heard. She was less than three years old, but she had no trouble remembering it. Another man remembered helping his father with a project at age four. Interestingly, he and his father were not particularly close at that time. The important fact was the matter of helping. His life was centered around helping others. His greatest frustrations came from hindrances to the help he wanted to give others.

Early recollections seem to assist in making a diagnosis of a problem because the ability to recall involves the ability to formulate a means for communication. One must be conscious of an event and be able to formulate the concept consciously to be able to recall it. It seems that people sometimes formulate those conscious concepts first with those things most important to them.

When studying early recollections, the details are not as important as the entire picture of the concept. For example, one woman recalled her presence at the death of her mother, and other people taking her mother's body away. The central concept was not death or her own feelings at the time. The central issue was one of important people leaving her. One way I have found helpful in trying to interpret early recollections is to try to formulate a participle to describe the event, for example, helping, leaving, being angry.

At this point Freud would include dreams as an important factor in diagnosis. In a few instances dreams can be helpful. Sometimes dreams are the reason people come to talk to their pastor. One lady, Evelyn, came to the office unannounced because she was troubled by a dream she had two nights earlier. In her dream, her husband, who had been dead for years, was sitting at the kitchen table the way he always had when he was alive. Her son wanted to do something, and Evelyn wanted and got her husband's advice in her dream. In reality, her son was about to take an action as an adult that frightened Evelyn, and she wanted to express her concern. She didn't know how to express it. She was satisfied that her dream was merely a subconscious effort to have her husband back to help her with her problem.

The case of the boy who suffered from nightmares and sleep terrors is another matter. His dreams were his problem. At first he could not remember them. He was suppressing them instead of dealing with them. His efforts to bring them to mind were helpful both from the standpoint of working against suppression and working toward resolution. When he could remember one dream he could remember more. All the details were different, but vivid. Yet, in spite of the variety of details, the plot was always the same. As in the case of early recollections, the plot is usually more important than the details.

A method of diagnostic procedure that is standard among professional counselors and almost wholly ignored among pastors and teachers is the method of starting with the worst possibility imaginable and then ruling out items one by one. Most pastors I have spoken with follow the opposite procedure. They begin with the simple presenting problem only to find that the matter is worse than they thought it was.

The frustrations and fears this causes can be reduced by looking first at the worst case scenario to find things can only get better. A man may go to the doctor because he is losing weight. Both he and the doctor know the real concern is that a malignancy may be present. Rather than starting with nutritional guidance, the doctor will probably do testing to rule out the presence of a malignancy. We can do the same thing in obtaining a diagnosis of an emotional problem. If a husband and wife are having problems, we may suspect one or the other has an alcohol or substance abuse problem. We may suspect an extramarital affair. Guided questions can rule out these possibilities while bringing others to light. This process is much easier on pastors or teachers than watching a situation deteriorate into a major problem before their eyes. By following this process, either you have identified the problem immediately, or things are not as serious as you thought they were.

Many other techniques could be added to this list, but these are some I have found most helpful in arriving at a conclusion about the real underlying problem. We can use them to whatever extent they prove beneficial, as long as they do not become an end in themselves. We may become very good at diagnosing a problem, but if we forget that resolution is the goal, we will not advance beyond diagnosis.

KNOW YOUR OWN LIMITATIONS

This is not what we can call one of the tricks of the trade. Pastors and teachers are fragile clay jars intended to hold the precious truth God pours into them. Our own spiritual lives are extremely important in doing this work. Counseling can be taxing and demanding. Many good pastoral counselors are particularly sensitive people and consequently likely to damage themselves spiritually, emotionally and even physically by doing such intensive work. We not only need the word of God to know what our people need to hear, we need it ourselves.

In professional circles, psychotherapists in training always go through a period of psychotherapy as part of their training. They need to know themselves. While we might not agree with the psychotherapy or its conclusions and resolutions, we can learn something from this principle. We will not only benefit from learning additional ways to counsel, but from being counseled by other people who can speak God's word to us on the level we would speak it. I believe more of this help for pastors would go far to eliminate some of the burnout and frustration, the fears and the disappointments they experience, and, ultimately, cut down the loss of pastors and teachers to our service.

Sadly, we often feel we know the gospel's answers better than anyone else. We shouldn't have these kinds of problems ourselves. That is not the point. Perhaps we do know God's word better than another counselor, but we still need to hear it all again and again just as our people do. One lady in the hospital put it succinctly. She said, "Thank you, Pastor, I needed that. I knew it already, but I needed to hear it again, especially now."

The professional field has a luxury we do not have. A professional counselor can refer people to someone else. We are usually dealing with members of the congregations we have been called to serve. If we fail to serve them with the gospel in the counseling ministry, if we tell them something they do not want to hear, if we are insensitive to their needs, we do not lose clients, we lose members. More important, someone may be lost to the holy Christian church. That is a tremendous responsibility to carry. Jesus never intended for us to carry it alone.

In some cases our own feelings may get in the way of doing what needs to be done. Some persons we counsel may have personality traits that make them difficult to work with. Some may be very demanding. Some may have been involved in sins that are difficult for us to cope with because of personal experiences. Professionals in these situations usually refer. A referral will be better for the client and easier on the counselor. We may not have that luxury. If we don't, we must know ourselves well enough to understand where our own feelings and emotions and experiences are getting in the way of resolution.

A pastor, for example, may have a strong commitment to his wife and his marriage. Pastors frequently hear about lack of commitment these days. Rather than sharing the importance of the marriage commitment, a pastor may let his own feelings get in the way. He may resent the lack of commitment, and work with the situation as if it were hopeless anyway.

All of us know what happens when we talk to people who have recently had surgery. Often these people only want to talk about their operation and show you their scars. The same thing can happen in counseling. Other people come in with problems, and the pastor immediately identifies them with something he is working out personally. This does not benefit the people who need help, and it usually does not benefit the pastor or teacher either. I have had people say, "I don't know how you can stand to listen to other people's problems all the time." My stock answer has become, "I enjoy hearing about other people's problems and working with them. I can go home thankful they're not my problems."

In the ministry we have tools, powerful tools for doing our work. No amount of training or experience will equip us better than the tools we already have for producing resolution. No power we have is greater than the power of God working through us as we declare his word.

That fact alone, however, demands excellence in our proficiency in this work. We will get better at it when we do the work more. Experience is a good teacher. The secular field, however, with its much more limited tools, has done a great deal to improve on techniques for getting their message out. Those techniques are usually not complicated or difficult to learn. They have a place in our work of seeking resolution. They can be handmaids, and they deserve some attention, whether we choose to take them or leave them.

CHAPTER TWELVE
THE EVIDENCE OF RESOLUTION

The evidence of resolution is one of the most rewarding parts of the work. At this point we can begin to understand better what kind of joy the angels of God experience when a sinner comes to repentance. Repentance, in fact, is the evidence of resolution. If we remember the definition of repentance, literally speaking, we are talking about a change of mind. The change of mind shows in many ways, but for our purposes we will summarize four of them. First, a person whose problem has been resolved by the gospel will no longer seek other forms of attempted resolution. Second, a person whose problem has been resolved by the gospel will demonstrate the peace of God that passes all understanding. Third, a person whose problem has been resolved by the gospel will seek whatever means are within his capabilities to correct any damage he has done with his problem. Fourth, a person whose problem has been resolved by the gospel will recognize that his problem itself can be a great asset in correcting his future. Once he has learned to take his personal trip to the cross, he may recognize more easily that he can do the same thing with other problems.

The person whose problem has been resolved by the gospel will no longer seek other forms of attempted resolution. Very often those other attempted forms of resolution and their consequent failures are the reason why a person comes for help in the first place. For example, drinking may be the problem, but drinking is only an attempt to resolve something else. Anger with another person may be a reason for talking with a counselor, but the anger is not the problem. The problem is what is causing the anger.

Many agencies, hospitals, and inpatient and outpatient settings are available for dealing with substance abuse. In many cases we believe we are doing the best and the most we can if we can just get a person to admit himself or herself to such a program. Recently I have become more convinced that we must deal with the reason for the drinking before taking that step because the agencies are incapable of dealing with it at the root.

When a person goes through such a program, he or she comes out free (we hope) of the abuse problem. He or she consequently no longer feels the need to resolve the underlying issue. You are not likely to see the person again in counseling because the behavior has changed, and the problem is out of the lives of the person and those closest to the problem. But that does not mean the root problem is solved Consider the example of Bill whom we met in chapter three.

When we take pains to find out what the underlying problem is before admission to a program we can actually eliminate the emotional needs to abuse substances. Success in a program thus becomes much more likely. We are much less likely to see a Pharisee emerging from the program, who has pulled himself up by his own bootstraps.

We have seen examples of people who no longer need to drink to resolve their problems, people who no longer need to be angry to resolve their problems, no longer need to punish themselves emotionally or physically to resolve their problems. The reason the need no longer exists is that these people have gone through the process of seeing God resolve their problems for them. They have not only seen the ineffectiveness of their own attempts and learned to recognize those attempts, they have seen the effectiveness of Christ's work done for them. Most likely they already knew the answers to their problems from some form of Christian training, but they had not applied them to themselves and their own situations because they couldn't see the applications. Christian counseling and gospel resolution simply assist them in making those applications.

One lady told me she had no idea Christ fit into so many parts of her life. She had learned to see him at work in parts of her life where she never thought of looking for him before. What more could a pastor ask as an indication that God's promise is true and God's gospel works?

A person whose problem has been resolved by the gospel will demonstrate the peace of God that passes all understanding. The most dramatic evidence of such peace I have ever seen was the case of the lady we met who suffered from paranoia. She was paranoid and her paranoia disappeared with resolution. Even more dramatically, the first time she laid her guilt down at the cross of Christ, the anxiety she had been experiencing disappeared, and the medication she was taking for anxiety became too much for her to treat her anxiety properly. She practically fell asleep in the office, although she hadn't been able to sleep well for weeks, even with the assistance of the medication.

Usually the evidence of resolution and peace is not that dramatic. A person may simply show more calm or even express a new calm he has not experienced for some time. One time when a man was in the hospital with ulcers, his improvement was significant in a very short period of time. His doctor asked how much pain he was experiencing. The man said the pain was much less significant. Finally the man asked, "How much pain will I have to live with?" The doctor replied that he should experience no pain. The man had been used to living with the pain and found it hard to believe he would live without it. Soon he had no pain at all. That was medical resolution. The same thing happens with gospel resolution. People who have been in emotional pain for years may find it hard to believe they can live without it. When they first experience it, it seems like a miracle. The truth is, it is a miracle only God can work.

A person whose problem has been resolved by the gospel will seek whatever means are within his capabilities to correct any damage he has done with his problem. Anger, resentment, bitterness, inconveniences caused to others, pain inflicted on others are the name of the game where emotional problems are concerned. People who are in emotional pain or physical pain themselves often try to shift the pain so others can walk in their shoes and experience their pain with them. The resulting marital problems, relational problems, physical problems and the like are numerous.

When a person's problem has been resolved by the gospel, he or she hardly needs to be told to straighten out matters with others who have been hurt by what they have done. Ann, for example, couldn't wait to get home to tell her children how good God had been to all of them. Connie couldn't wait to ask her husband's forgiveness for all she had put him and the family through.

Gospel resolution and subsequent fruits of repentance have clear biblical precedence. Zaccheus didn't need to be told to restore what he had stolen as a tax collector. The woman taken in adultery hardly had to be told that Jesus expected her to change her behavior. Every indication is that she had all the motivation she needed to make sure adultery was not a part of her life in the future.

These kinds of changes of mind are much more significant than mere modifications of behavior patterns. Behavior modification is more like treating symptoms rather than root causes. Consequently, those changes in behavior are much less rewarding than seeing God change a heart and a mind and produce sanctification, as only God can, according to the law's direction.

The first time one experiences this kind of resolution, it's almost hard to believe God could have done it. After a while, a pastor, teacher or counselor begins to realize his work is not done until he sees the evidence of resolution. In some cases, of course, no external evidence is possible. If, for example, a person still holds onto guilt for something that happened years before and cannot be undone, the repentance and evidence will take place in the person alone. He or she can do nothing for the offended person.

One lady spoke of twenty years of guilt she had experienced because of a premarital sexual relationship. She could and did talk the matter through with her understanding and forgiving husband, but she could not change what she had done. The evidence of her resolution was finally appropriating God's forgiveness for herself, something she had always been unable to do.

This leads to the fourth evidence of resolution. *A person whose problem has been resolved by the gospel will recognize his problem itself can be a great asset in correcting future situations.*

The lady who talked about her premarital sexual affair, for example, said, "If I have experienced this kind of guilt over what happened twenty years ago, if I have buried it in my mind where I didn't have to think about it for years, can you imagine how I would feel if I had an extramarital affair now? I couldn't do it." She sounded a lot like we would expect the woman to sound to whom Jesus said, "Neither do I condemn you." Besides that, she had a renewed understanding of how important it was to give her own daughter directions and controls that would help her keep from making the same mistakes she had made.

When God said he will make all things work together for good to those who love him and are called according to his purpose, he was talking about gospel resolution. He was talking about people who live in and by his love. He was talking about us and our people. He was talking about people who have firsthand experience of God's love and forgiveness.

The example of the Apostle Paul has always been helpful to me. I have often told people: "Paul never forgot he had been a persecutor of the church of Christ, but God forgot." Paul's suffering was never a punishment for the converted persecutor, it was something God allowed him to experience to understand the glories of God better. His thorn in the flesh was never a reminder from God that Paul had persecuted the church, it was God's loving way of keeping him humbly dependent on God for the strength and power he needed. Paul was only a human being and was forced to remember so by the thorn in his old sinful flesh. That he had been a persecutor of the church only motivated him to do more in service to Christ because of Christ's mercy and forgiveness.

After seeing the evidence of gospel resolution occurring time and again, we may begin to take it for granted and come to the point where we believe we have actually accomplished it. About that time something usually indicates that we have no control over obtaining this resolution. We can present the gospel, we can be as effective as possible in making the presentation, we can also be persistent in it. But God is the one who produces the results.

In counseling, just as in every other aspect of the ministry, people have the awesome and terrible ability to reject what God is offering them. Even the secular counseling field is aware that many people refuse to be helped no matter how much help is available. That resistance is even more apparent when working with the gospel, which goes contrary to human nature itself. The human nature neither wants nor trusts help from the enemy, God. Nevertheless, the evidence of resolution is a privilege God allows us to see time and again, so we know his gospel works. Every human invention, on the other hand, produces only a cheap imitation of resolution.

CHAPTER THIRTEEN
THE MAINTENANCE OF RESOLUTION

As we have come to understand resolution through these chapters, clearly gospel resolution will only take place when the gospel is presented. This involves much more than the simple assurance of forgiveness in Christ. It involves using the law to reveal not only surface sins, but deep-seated, underlying sins and guilt. It means addressing those sins when they are recognized by the troubled sinner. It means confronting them with the process of redemption. It means going through the process the Apostle Paul describes so eloquently in 2 Corinthians 5, where he shows how God made Christ the sinner so we could be made the righteous. That is gospel resolution. The process continues with accumulated evidence of resolution or, speaking dogmatically, through sanctification.

Once the process of resolution has become evident, can we actually say it has been completed? Hardly. We are not doing battle with mere emotional difficulties, behavior problems and broken relationships. We are doing battle with the sinful flesh. That sinful flesh is an enemy, first, because it wills to return to the same sins. It is an enemy, second, because it opposes the resolution the gospel provides, even after that resolution has been experienced. Time and again people who have gone through the process and resolved their problems fail to return when the problem begins to recur. On numerous occasions people have returned only after seeking secular counseling, and have paid dearly for it, only to long for the resolution they experienced before.

A pastor or teacher may warn people that they will have problems again. Their thoughts will recur. Their mistaken ways of dealing with their problems will continue to suggest themselves as alternatives. Pastors and teachers can encourage these people who have experienced gospel resolution to come for help before the situation gets out of hand again. Some will come. Many will not come until they reach the point of unbearable pain once again. The reason for this kind of hesitation is, again, that we are not only doing battle with the problems themselves, we are doing battle with the sinful flesh itself. Add to the sinful flesh a society seeking peace anywhere but from the gospel, and our people will go along for the ride.

When radio personalities offer solutions to daily problems over the air, our people are just as inclined as anyone else to go along with the crowd and think they are getting real spiritual food. Those who have experienced the resolution the gospel gives are more likely to sense a shallow and hollow message when they hear it than those who have not experienced the resolution. Nevertheless, the alternative channels to gospel resolution are numerous and tempting.

One of the most important things we can do to maintain gospel resolution is to stand ready to give "refresher courses," assuring people, without being pessimistic, that they will need a refresher. "When this happens again, don't wait. Let me know. Let me know how things are going. Let me know whether things are still as good as they are now. Let me know when things get worse."

People who have gone through all that is involved in gospel resolution know it is intensive work both for themselves and their pastor, teacher or counselor. Sometimes people believe they will be too much of a burden. Perhaps they have already used more than they consider their fair share of the counselor's time. They think they will be doubling their debt if they come back. They think they should be able to handle the situation themselves. They are disappointed in themselves more than anything else.

Many times I have assured people that it is more difficult for me not to meet with them than it is to find the time to meet. For one thing, the problems usually increase instead of getting better. Similarly, a concerned pastor wants to be available to his people, and, when they don't come, he can't help wondering why. Not dealing with people's problems is much more difficult than dealing with them.

A pastor or teacher will want to follow up on work that has reached resolution. Usually this is easily done with a simple question in church when greeting people at the door. One time I asked a lady at the door when she was leaving church, "Are you all right? You look like something is bothering you." That was enough to prompt her to call in appreciation for the concern expressed and it opened the door to resolution of a problem no one would have thought this lady had. The scene recurs time and again.

When people have been working together as intensively as counseling situations demand, they gain the ability to sense problems even without much evidence that problems exist. This kind of sensitivity helps many troubled people to come for refresher courses instead of seeking other, imitation resolutions.

On one occasion, a mother who had been through many problems with her daughter called to say she was seeing evidence of some of the same problems. What could be done about it? I suggested that resolution would not be difficult because her daughter had clearly understood the process before. The mother was skeptical, but we agreed on a meeting time. The meeting with mother, daughter and myself lasted a little more than an hour. This mother thought she was seeing a miracle take place before her eyes as she watched her daughter begin to relax, to smile, to talk openly and to exhibit peace. Without a doubt this mother was experiencing a miracle. She was experiencing God's miracle of gospel resolution taking place. I have to admit that I was not as amazed as she was. I had seen her daughter experience it much more dramatically before. In only an hour she was back to the same peace she had gained several months earlier. The first time the process took six weeks. This time it took one hour.

Many people expect to get the same thing from a counseling agency that they would get from a gospel-based church. This holds true as much for those who have experienced gospel resolution as those who have not. Usually those who have heard and come to understand the application of the law and the gospel will soon recognize the shallowness of other organizations and agencies, even some called Christian. We do well, therefore, to help our people find truly Christian counselors and, by all means, to keep our own doors open and ready for our people whenever they need us.

One young man had come for counseling and had been able, with the help of God, to resolve his problem. It had been a time-consuming process. When the problems began to recur and to show themselves in other ways he sought help from a Christian counseling agency. He had sessions weekly for almost a year before returning for his refresher course. It became clear almost immediately that this young man was carrying a heavy burden of guilt. Nevertheless, he had been with this so-called Christian counseling agency for a year and had become frustrated because they never dealt with his guilt at all. When I asked him how they had suggested he deal with his feelings of guilt, he told me they had given him a book on children of alcoholics and the guilt they experience. Once again God resolved his guilt, but in this case the help he had sought elsewhere actually doubled the amount of time it took to reach that resolution.

Another man worked through a school with a post-graduate program in psychology to resolve his personal problems. Most of his time was spent either with students or with a non-directive counselor. He had spent two years with this program and was more frustrated than when he began. By the time he came for help he allowed me six weeks to resolve the problem, or he was determined to give up altogether. Again, his previous counseling experience had greatly hindered the resolution of his problems.

If we are to help our people maintain the resolution God has provided for them, the most important thing we can do is to let them know that nothing but the word of God can accomplish resolution. The mere title, "Christian," does not guarantee they will be getting the same thing from those agencies that they will get from their church home. "Christian," often only means "relatively moral" in the face of all kinds of humanistic and immoral psychotherapies. Unfortunately, "Christian" does not necessarily mean law and gospel centered and based, any more than the term "Lutheran" guarantees a person's commitment to the teachings of Luther and the confessions based on the word of God. On the other hand, when "Christian" does mean law and gospel oriented, pastors and teachers will welcome the presence and work of other Christian counselors.

When pastors and teachers get to know their people on an individual basis the way counseling allows, they will be affected by the experience. Many times experiences repeat themselves with different counseling cases. Several years ago our area suffered from widespread unemployment. Dozens of people came for counseling with the same problem. Their image of themselves was shattered because their income was cut off or drastically reduced. Their self-worth was at an all-time low because many had based their self-worth on their ability to earn a good wage.

This difficult period offered an excellent opportunity to teach people that their self-worth was determined by what God was willing and able to do for them in Christ, not by what they were able to do for themselves and their families. That recurring theme, without even planning it, became the application of many sermons. A pastor cannot spend twenty or thirty hours a week talking about the same thing with people individually, and fail to realize that other people he is not seeing privately may have the same problems. In short, sermons became much more meaningful and personal for the entire congregation because of the individual contacts we had with people in their personal lives.

This leads us to the primary and most effective way of maintaining gospel resolution. If anything keeps sermons from being impersonal and dogmatic in the negative sense, it is personal contact with people who are experiencing difficulties only the gospel can resolve. Because of the personal experiences I have had seeing gospel resolution at work, I have almost stopped talking about forgiveness by itself. I have replaced the simple words, "You are forgiven," with a trip to the cross and a declaration of redemption that many of the people in the congregation have experienced alone in the office in a counseling session.

The preaching of the law is much more personal and direct when speaking to particular sins and sins that lie under the surface. The declaration of justification by grace through faith is addressed to the world, and it is addressed to *you*. Our preaching will almost naturally become more personal and more direct when we have spoken to people individually, and then declare the same truths publicly.

If you talk to one person privately about a particular sin and see the gospel resolution for it at work, statistically you will have twenty people out of a hundred who will be able to relate to the same thing. If one person hears what you told him or her in the office three days earlier, twenty people will tell you, if they take the time to do it, that you must have been talking directly to them in your sermon. That means you have a weekly opportunity to maintain gospel resolution for those who have experienced it, and a weekly opportunity to provide it for those who have not experienced it in a counseling session.

According to national statistics, forty people out of every one hundred need some sort of counseling. Only twenty percent of that forty percent get the help they need in counseling. But if our preaching and teaching are actually counseling sessions to the masses, we don't have to do individual counseling with all the people with the same problems. We can reach them from the pulpit or in the class.

This will serve to accomplish two important things. It may first reduce the amount of time we need to spend doing personal counseling and, more important, it may increase the amount of counseling we do because people recognize we understand and are concerned about their problems. Besides that, 100% of our people need what the law and gospel offer. They may not all need it from us on a special and personal basis, but they all need it. While national statistics concern only those who have behavioral problems, we are concerned with the sin problem, and that is universal. The gospel is the universal factor in genuine resolution. We have the privilege of using it both publicly and privately. Both public and private declaration will improve as we work to obtain and maintain gospel resolution.

CHAPTER FOURTEEN
THE JOY OF RESOLUTION
FOR PASTOR AND PEOPLE

For reasons known only to the individuals involved, counseling is often one area where pastors and teachers feel inadequate and incompetent in doing their work. For reasons too numerous to mention, our people may not expect to find competent counseling capabilities in the office of the pastor or teacher. Because of such feelings and beliefs, we may be discouraging each other from doing more than we are doing in this area. Pastors and teachers may be expressing their inadequacies without realizing it, or even intentionally. Our people may be expressing the idea that we don't need to be doing more because other means and agencies are better equipped to do it.

By now we should be aware that our people need the resolution of the gospel in dealing with their problems, no matter how simple or complex they are. No one who lacks a thorough understanding of the law and gospel has the equipment for providing resolution. If we are not ready and willing to stand up for counseling with the law and gospel as much as we are ready to stand up and preach and teach the law and gospel, we are literally sending our people to others who likely cannot give them the resolution Christ won for them.

At times we may need professional assistance and direction. At times we may need the counsel of the medical and psychological professions to let us know just how serious problems may be. At times we may need and want additional training to be able to communicate law and gospel more efficiently. The love we have for the word of God that brought us into our ministries in the first place is enough motive to obtain all the proficiency we can obtain to share it. Our love for the Savior who loved us enough to save us and give us the good news to share is sufficient to motivate us to do the best job we can in sharing it in every facet of the ministry.

Yes, there will be disappointments. Some will walk away from what we have to offer the same way many disciples walked away to walk no more with Jesus. Yes, others will put it off the way Felix put off the Apostle Paul until a convenient time that never came. Many of the people in your congregation may be willing to spend hundreds and thousands of dollars for counseling and professional help that only the gospel can give, instead of accepting what you can give them without charge. Some may even die with their problems, refusing to allow the gospel to accomplish resolution.

Similar disappointments happen in every facet of the ministry. They are part of our evangelism work, our preaching, our teaching, our delinquent work. But the setbacks don't prevent us from doing those parts of our ministry. Neither should some failures and disappointments keep us from carrying on individualized counseling in our ministries.

God has given us his law and gospel. How can we justifiably say we are not equipped to do this work? God has equipped us. God has promised to bless the individual proclamation of his law and gospel as much as he has promised to bless the public proclamation of it. His power to resolve the problems and turmoils our people experience is just as great in the counseling office as it is in the pulpit. The Savior's redemptive work that *has taken all sin away* is just as important to declare personally and individually as it is publicly. That is what Jesus won. No one who says less than that is really preaching the gospel.

We know what the blessings are that Jesus has won. His life, death and resurrection have closed hell and opened heaven. His work established peace with God, no matter what Satan tries to do to deny it. God never promised life would be easy for Christians. In fact, Psalm 73 indicates what many Christians already know, namely, that sometimes life seems harder for a Christian than for those who aren't Christians. But what do those without Christ have to look forward to? Paul makes it clear in Romans 8 that suffering is a part of living, but we don't have to suffer alone. 2 Corinthians 12 shows that God understands the individual needs of his people and provides just the right individual way to keep us close to him. He may use thorns in the flesh to help accomplish that. But in every one of these instances, God in Christ and his full and free forgiveness is the answer, the hope and the strength.

As we share that with our people now publicly, we know we have a privilege even the angels of heaven have not been given. Our sins have been paid for, and so have those of our people. Our work is to say so, thoroughly and personally.

In the counseling session we can address one specific sin, when we see it, and watch God resolve it. We can see peace in the eyes of the people who avail themselves of the opportunity to experience it. We can talk to a

Zacchaeus, the woman taken in adultery, the Samaritan woman at Jacob's well, the Ethiopian, Elijah, Moses, Jonah, David and all the others God dealt with individually to produce resolution. Besides that we can talk to the thousands (or hundreds or dozens as the case may be) together, the way the apostles spoke to the people on Pentecost.

Most important, by the grace of God, through this effective means of individual counseling, we can look forward with the same joy we have in the hope in Christ that prompts us to preach and teach the gospel publicly. We can look forward to sharing with our people the joy of resolution Christ has won. That joy belongs to us now and forever. We have the privilege of knowing that we have a small part in sharing the resolution secured when Christ died on the cross and rose from the grave. That's gospel resolution and nothing else can compare with it. God help us do everything we can, not to be satisfied or allow our people to be satisfied with less than Christ won for us in the gospel for resolution. God help us to do all our COUNSELING AT THE CROSS.

APPENDIX

The following is a list of encoded messages that could warn of suicidal danger if taken together or in a suicidal context. The list is presented by Marv Miller, PhD and William Wargo, PhD through THE INFORMATION CENTER, 11036 Ironwood Road, San Diego, CA 92131. The booklet is entitled, *The Suicide Intervention Training Manual,* copyright 1990. (Used by permission.)

1. "I've decided to kill myself."

2. "I've had it. I'm through."

3. "I wish I were dead."

4. "I'm not the man I used to be."

5. "I've lived long enough."

6. "I'm calling it quits—it's useless."

7. "I hate my life. I hate everyone and everything."

8. "It was good at times, but we all have to say good-bye."

9. "The only way out is for me to die."

10. "I just can't go on any longer."

11. "You won't be seeing me around anymore."

12. "Do you believe in reincarnation? I'd like to come back someday. Maybe things will be better then."

13. "If I don't see you again, thanks for everything."

14. "You're going to regret how you've treated me."

15. "It's too much to put up with."

16. "Life has lost its meaning for me."

17. "Nobody needs me anymore."

18. "I have a premonition. I'm going far away on a long trip."

19. "I'm thinking seriously about making out my will." (Said by a 24-year-old pregnant woman with two children)

20. "I'm getting out. I'm tired of life."

21. "Ever since I've retired, I've felt in the way all the time."

22. "Do you know the procedure for donating your eyes after death?"

23. "How do they preserve your kidneys for transplantation if you die suddenly?"

24. "I wish I could tell you how important you've been. You've helped me see things clearly. Now I know the only road that's open for me."

25. "Life is like a short circuit. There's a sputter, then the lights go out."

26. "If (such and such) happens, I'll kill myself."

27. "If (such and such) doesn't happen, I'll kill myself."

28. "You know, son, I'm going home soon."

29. "Here, take this (cherished possession). I won't be needing it anymore."

BIBLIOGRAPHY

Adams, Jay E. *Competent to Counsel.* Nutley, N.J.: Presbyterian and Reformed Publishing, 1976.

American Psychiatric Association. *Diagnostic and Statistical Manual of Mental Disorders—Third Edition-Revised (DSM-III R), 1987.*

Anastasi, Anne. *Psychological Testing.* New York, N.Y.: Macmillan, 1988.

Becker, Siegbert W. *The Scriptures—Inspired of God.* Milwaukee, Wis.: Northwestern, 1971.

Beitman, Bernard D. *The Structure of Individual Psychotherapy.* New York, N.Y.: Guilford Press, 1987.

Bobgan, Martin and Diedre. *How to Counsel from Scripture.* Chicago, Ill.: Moody Press, 1985.

Bobgan, Martin and Deidre. *Psychoheresy.* Santa Barbara, Cal.: Eastgate, 1987.

Browne, Angela. *When Battered Women Kill.* New York: The Fortress Press, Macmillan, 1987.

Bugleski and Graziano. *The Handbook of Practical Psychology.* Englewood Cliffs, N.J.: Prentice Hall, 1980.

Burns, David D. *Feeling Good.* New York: William Morrow, 1980.

Buscaglia, Leo F. *Living, Loving and Learning.* New York: Ballantine Books, 1982.

Capps, Donald. *Biblical Approaches to Pastoral Counseling.* Philadelphia, Penn.: Westminster Press, 1981.

BIBLIOGRAPHY

Carson, Butcher, Coleman. *Abnormal Psychology and Modern Life.* Glenview, Ill.: Scott Foresman, 1988.

Clinebell, Howard. *Basic Types of Pastoral Care and Counseling.* Nashville, Tenn.: Abingdon Press, 1984.

Cobb, John B. Jr. *Theology and Pastoral Care.* Philadelphia, Penn.: Fortress Press, 1977.

Collins, Gary R. *Innovative Approaches to Counseling.* Waco, Tx.: Word, 1986.

Collins, Gary R. *Psychology & Theology.* Nashville, Tenn.: Abingdon Press, 1981.

Corsini, Raymond J., ed. *Current Psychotherapies.* Itasca, Ill.: F. E. Peacock 1979.

Crabb, Lawrence J. Jr. *Basic Principles of Biblical Counseling.* Grand Rapids, Mich.: Zondervan, 1975.

Crabb, Lawrence J. Jr. *Effective Biblical Counseling.* Grand Rapids, Mich.: Zondervan, 1977.

Crabb, Lawrence J. Jr. *How to Become One with Your Mate.* Grand Rapids, Mich.: Zondervan, 1982.

Crabb, Lawrence J. Jr. *Inside Out.* Colorado Springs, Col.: Navpress, 1988.

Crabb, Lawrence J. Jr. *The Marriage Builder.* Grand Rapids, Mich.: Zondervan, 1982.

Crabb, Lawrence J. Jr. *Understanding People.* Grand Rapids, Mich.: Zondervan, 1987.

Dobson, James C. *Dare to Discipline.* Wheaton, Ill.: Tyndale, 1972.

Dobson, James C. *Hide and Seek.* Old Tappan, N.J.: Fleming H. Revell, 1979.

Dobson, James C. *Love Must Be Tough.* Waco, Tx.: Word, 1983.

Dobson, James C. *Preparing for Adolescence.* Ventura, Calif.: Regal Books, 1980.

Dobson, James C. *Straight Talk to Men and Their Wives.* Waco, Tx.: Word, 1984.

Dobson, James C. *The Strong-Willed Child.* Wheaton, Ill.: Regal Books, 1986.

Ellis, Albert. *Growth through Reason.* North Hollywood, Calif.: Wilshire Book Co., 1971.

Glasser, William. *Control Theory.* New York, N.Y.: Harper & Row, 1984.

Haas, Harold J. *The Christian Encounters Mental Illness.* St. Louis, Mo.: Concordia, 1966.

Hart, Archibald. *Adrenalin & Stress.* Waco, Tx.: Word Books, 1986.

Hart, Archibald. *Coping With Depression in the Ministry and Other Helping Professions.* Waco, Tx.: Word Books, 1984.

Helzer and Guze. *Psychiatry.* 5 vols. St. Louis, Mo.: Basic Books, 1986.

Hulme, William E. *Pastoral Care and Counseling.* Minneapolis, Minn.: Augsburg, 1981.

Hyder, O. Q. *The Christian's Handbook of Psychiatry.* Old Tappan, N.J.: Spire Books, 1977.

Johnson, Craig and Connors, Mary E. *The Etiology and Treatment of Bulimia Nervosa.* New York, N.Y.: Basic Books, Inc., 1987.

Jung, C. G. *Psychology and Religion.* New Haven: Yale University Press, 1938.

Kaplan, Freedman, Sadock. *Comprehensive Textbook of Psychiatry/IV.* 2 vols. Baltimore, Md.: Williams and Wilkins, 1985.

Kelsey, Morton T. *Christo-Psychology.* New York: Crossroads, 1982.

Koehler, Walter J. *Counseling and Confession.* St. Louis, Mo.: Concordia, 1982.

LaHaye, Tim. *Spirit-Controlled Temperament.* Wheaton, Ill.: Tyndale, 1966.

LaHaye, Tim. *Transformed Temperaments.* Wheaton, Ill.: Tyndale, 1974.

Leman, Kevin. *The Birth Order Book.* New York, N.Y.: Dell, 1985.

Lyon. H. Curtis. *The Holy Scripture as Source and Norm for Doctrine and Practice in Pastoral Counseling and Psychology.* Thesis for STM, Wisconsin Lutheran Seminary, 1987.

Menninger, Carl, M.D. *Whatever Became of Sin?* New York: Hawthorn Books, 1973.

Miller, Marvin. *1989 Training Workshop Manual.* Solana Beach, Calif.: The Information Center, 1989.

Minuchin and Fishman. *Family Therapy Techniques.* Cambridge, Mass.: Harvard, 1981.

Napier and Whitaker. *The Family Crucible.* New York: Harper and Row, 1978.

Narramore, Bruce. *Help, I'm a Parent.* Grand Rapids, Mich.: Zondervan, 1972.

Narramore, Clyde M. *Encyclopedia of Psychological Problems*. Grand Rapids, Mich.: Zondervan, 1966.

Narramore, Clyde M. *The Psychology of Counseling*. Grand Rapids, Mich.: Zondervan, 1960.

Nicholi, Armand M., Jr., M.D. *The New Harvard Guide to Psychiatry*. Cambridge, Mass.: Harvard University Press, 1988.

Pastor as Counselor. Milwaukee, Wis.: Northwestern.

Pietrofeso, Hoffman, Splete, and Pinto. *Counseling: Theory, Research and Practice*. Boston, Mass.: Houghton, Mifflin, 1978.

Roberts, Albert. *Crisis Intervention Handbook*. Belmont, Calif.: Wadsworth, 1990.

Sarason and Sarason. *Abnormal Psychology*. Englewood Cliffs, N.J.: Prentice-Hall, 1984.

Schuetze and Matzke. *The Counseling Shepherd*. Milwaukee, Wis.: Northwestern, 1988.

Schuetze, A. and Habeck, I. *The Shepherd Under Christ*. Milwaukee, Wis.: Northwestern, 1974.

Schuller, Robert H. *Peace of Mind Through Possibility Thinking*. New York: Doubleday, 1977.

Schuller, Robert H. *Self-Esteem: The New Reformation*. Waco, Tx.: Word, 1982.

Shelley, Martin. *Helping Those Who Don't Want Help*. Waco, Tx.: Word, 1986.

Strupp and Binder. *Psychotherapy in a New Key*. New York: Basic Books, 1984.

Tournier, Paul. *A Place for You*. New York: Harper and Row, 1968.

Tournier, Paul. *Guilt and Grace*. New York: Harper and Row, 1962.

Tournier, Paul. *The Healing of Persons*. New York: Harper and Row, 1965.

Wilson, R. Reid. *Don't Panic*. New York, N.Y.: Harper & Row, 1986.

Witkin-Lanoil, Georgia. *The Male Stress Syndrome*. New York: New Market Press, 1986.

Wright, H. Norman. *How to Have a Creative Crisis*. Waco, Tx.: Word, 1986.

260979BV00003B/1/P

9 780810 003538